Notes from Walnut Tree Farm

ROGER DEAKIN

Edited by Alison Hastie and Terence Blacker

PENGUIN BOOKS

PENGUIN BOOKS

Published by the Penguin Group
Penguin Books Ltd, 80 Strand, London WC2R ORL, England
Penguin Group (USA) Inc., 375 Hudson Street, New York, New York 10014, USA
Penguin Group (Canada), 90 Eglinton Avenue East, Suite 700, Toronto, Ontario, Canada M4P 2Y3
(a division of Pearson Penguin Canada Inc.)
Penguin Ireland, 25 St Stephen's Green, Dublin 2, Ireland
(a division of Penguin Books Ltd)
Penguin Group (Australia), 250 Camberwell Road, Camberwell, Victoria 3124, Australia
(a division of Pearson Australia Group Pty Ltd)
Penguin Books India Pvt Ltd, 11 Community Centre, Panchsheel Park, New Delhi – 110 017, India
Penguin Group (NZ), 67 Apollo Drive, Rosedale, North Shore 0632, New Zealand
(a division of Pearson New Zealand Ltd)
Penguin Books (South Africa) (Pty) Ltd, 24 Sturdee Avenue, Rosebank, Johannesburg 2196, South Africa

Penguin Books Ltd, Registered Offices: 80 Strand, London WC2R ORL, England

www.penguin.com

First published by Hamish Hamilton 2008
Published in Penguin Books 2009
1

Printed in England by Clays Ltd, St Ives plc

ISBN: 978–0–141–03902–2

www.greenpenguin.co.uk

PENGUIN BOOKS

NOTES FROM WALNUT TREE FARM

'Roger Deakin was unique; he saw and felt the world like nobody else. *Notes from Walnut Tree Farm* is as remarkable and as affecting as anything John Muir wrote; in fact, I think it is this century's *Walden*. It might even be the best of his books; or perhaps there is no need to rank them like this. It completes the triptych, begun with *Waterlog* and *Wildwood*, in the most wonderful way'

Robert Macfarlane, author of *The Wild Places* and literary executor of the Roger Deakin Estate

Contents

Foreword

For the last six years of his life, Roger Deakin kept a record of his daily life, work, thoughts and memories. Forty-five lined exercise books were completed in his distinctive, bold handwriting. Each was numbered and paginated, with a table of contents carefully listed on the cover.

The entries themselves were altogether freer. Spontaneous, playful, impassioned and sometimes experimental, they were Roger's everyday observations, and reflected the events of his inner and outer life as they happened.

Some of the entries were research notes for *Wildwood*, the book he was writing at the time, or for one of his radio programmes, while others were written during his travels in Australia or Eastern Europe. Most of the contents, though, related to his life at Walnut Tree Farm, the extraordinary, much loved house in Suffolk where he lived for the last thirty years of his life. It is these entries which have provided the material for this book.

We have selected extracts from the notebooks, including dates when they were mentioned, and have arranged them month by month to form one composite year. Abbreviations have been expanded, but otherwise Roger's words have been allowed to speak for themselves.

Alison Hastie
Terence Blacker
July 2008

1st January

I am lying full length on my belly on frozen snow and frosty tussocks in the railway wood blowing like a dragon into the wigwam of a fire at the core of a tangled blackthorn bonfire. I am clearing the blackthorn suckers that march out from the hedge like the army in *Macbeth*, the marching wood, threatening to overwhelm the whole wood in their dense, spiny thicket.

The technique is to get right down on the ground and go in with the triangular bow-saw at ground level, then grab the cut stems and drag the bushes away to the bonfire, which grows like a giant porcupine, bristling with spines that inflict a particular, unforgettable ache in the hands and thumbs of the woodman.

The bonfire just keeps working itself up to a sudden burst of wildly crackling, spitting flame, and burning a chimney up its centre. Then it dies down, frosting the twigs with fire but failing to ignite with any conviction because the wood is too fresh, too green and sappy. It is exhausting work, crawling at

1

rabbit level through a blackthorn thicket and sawing through the tough little trunks. You realize why blackthorn was used defensively as a dead hedge by the Saxons; it is the true precursor of barbed wire.

I stumble back up the field for a tea-break to listen to myself on *Home Planet* on the radio and fall headlong in the snow by the shepherd's hut. Tracks everywhere in the snow, mostly rabbit, and a single bee orchid standing up with dried seeds in the snowy field.

A mauve, misty penumbra across the fields under a duck-egg sky and the glow of sunset. Everything very still and quiet.

2nd January
Another brilliant, intensely cold morning. Trees and everything enamelled and frosted, sparkling and frilly with frost.

Hard to get the car started – cold diesel and frozen windscreens. Put more antifreeze in the tractor. Then a snow drive over icy roads to see Ronnie Blythe at Bottengoms.

We have lunch in the Six Bells in Bures – cod and chips, and halves of Guinness – and set off to Ager Fen, where we walk through the ancient mixed woods of cherry, oak, fir, hazel, willow, poplar, ash. Ronnie says all country children were conceived in woods, because you couldn't make love in the house: there were too many people in there – children, parents, etc., no privacy at all. So you went to the woods.

Ronnie lends me John Masefield's thumb stick, carved by him and later, in Oxford, given to Dr 'Bird' Partridge – who in turn gave it to Ronnie.

Ronnie walks with a bird's claw stick of blackthorn that belonged to John Nash. A bird's foot clutches an egg of wood. Lovely.

There are warrens and dips where clay was quarried and then carted off for building – and there is a big wood bank running along the parish boundary.

Big ancient cherries with fungal bracelets.

Then on to Tiger Wood – so called because the tooth of a sabre-toothed tiger was once found there somewhere.

Ronnie says how much he loves the ruinousness of woods – of the dead trees fallen over each other. John Nash loved dead trees lying about, scattered. He didn't like woods to be tidied up too much.

There's a brick-maker's cottage in Tiger Wood, one of only two houses in the wood, surrounded by old brick-clay burrowings and pits. Every spring they have a bluebell party in the cottage and toast the bluebells and listen to the nightingales. There are about six pairs of nightingales in this wood, resting in Ager Fen.

Driving back through the rolling country to Wormingford, Ronnie points out that this was once all the deer park of the Waldegrave family, who are buried in the chapel on the hill top.

The bonfire is still burning under the crack willow by the common, smouldering and gently glowing, melting the snow that tries to settle on it, smoking just faintly.

Immense numbers of tits, mainly blue, a few great, the

occasional coal or marsh, on the three peanut cylinders. They are all over the damson tree, waiting their turn or digesting peanuts. All sorts of power groupings and petty struggles over who is king of the castle. Now here comes the spotted woodpecker, approaching cautiously through the damson branches. Sees a sudden movement of mine at the window, flees far across the meadow.

I cut a hazel-coppice pole out of my wood and used it as a curtain pole in my bedroom. It works well.

4th January

Walking up Stonebridge Lane with Jayne [Ivimey], I notice the width of the old stone bridge – twenty feet at least – I must dig it out and measure properly. As you walk the lane, you see how the farmers have all encroached and how the new middle-class squatters are claiming stakes on the lane, using it for horse jumps, etc. We walk on to the old ash pollard on Burgate Little Green, then on into Burgate Wood, passing a leaning chestnut pollard – a long, pendulous bough. Jayne remarks that trees are like people: you don't have to talk to them, but you get to recognize them all.

As the light changes, we depend more on our feet, on

feeling our way through the wood. Shapes of things loom up. A paleness in a covert seems at first to be water, a woodland pond, but turns out to be a fallen silver birch, a bold streak of white in the wood.

On the way out, on the lane to Burgate Hall, a metal paling has grown into the trunk of an ash. The iron bars of the fence pass straight through the middle of the trunk, like whirling dervishes in Kurdistan with knives through their bodies.

An old house may be built of the humblest, simplest materials, and, like a bird's nest, be a thing of great beauty.

Or: like a bird's nest, a house may be beautiful because of the way it combines the simple, ordinary natural materials of which it is built.

An early swim with Janine [Edge] and Helen Napper at Leiston Pool, then a big breakfast with porridge, sultanas and linseed soaked overnight in water (recipe by Helen Napper). Talk of a future walk in the woods with Madeleine [Wynn] and greyhounds and young chess-master Hugo. Then out to the sea to buy fish from a fisherman at a hut, a black-tarred pine hut with a radio inside wishing fishermen good fishing and giving the weather forecast. I bought a skate, a half pound of sprats and some cooked cod's roe. Newspaper cuttings on the door about Alzheimer's and fish-eating as a way to avoid it.

A walk along the beach to see Maggi Hambling's new oyster-shell sculpture: 'Hear those voices that will not be drowned.' These were the fishermen I filmed at Aldeburgh in 1997.

Then up the road to the ruined slate-roofed cottage on the marsh, and the apple tree in the shingle beach. All-round circumference of 100 ft, 23 ft in diameter, 3–4 ft high, very squat and dense. Already almost in bud in its bunker.

Thence to Thorpeness, like a film set – phony half-timbers, and a concrete church, like a toy-town. The artificial mere, the country club, the huge village hall, sports and social club.

I keep puzzling about that apple tree, buried up to its neck in the shingle like a daddy at the seaside. It can't quite see the sea. If it were to grow another ten feet, it could peep over the top of the long ridge of shingle that stretches from Aldeburgh to Thorpeness. It grows in the shelter of a bunker, a hollow in the dunes of shingle and sand that helps protect it from the wind. I suppose the sheer withering intensity of the wind must prune the budding twigs relentlessly so that the tree takes the only course of survival left open to it: to creep ever outwards, crouching low and close to the shingle, creating a pincushion of densely branched fruiting spurs.

I have seen people gathering apples from it in summer. Outside the seasons of flowers and fruit, most people would pass it by, mistaking it for a scrubby sallow bush. No doubt the salt spray of winter gales must provide the tree with an antifungal dusting that may well be helping to keep it healthy. It must be a relic of an ancient orchard, perhaps connected with the derelict cottage a hundred yards inland that looks across the marshes. Somewhere down there the roots are finding fresh water. But this still must count as one of the hardiest apple trees in Britain.

At Ubbeston I walked a green lane that has long beckoned to be explored. The coastal sunshine had given way to a uniform bleak grey, a cold wind and occasional bouts of rain. I trudged uphill on a wide grassy track between old hedges with the occasional oak pollard, tousle-mopped, no longer regularly cut. In contrast to the oaks nearer the coast, these trees were in healthy enough condition. All along the edge of the sandlings, where the heavier Suffolk claylands begin as you head inland, the parkland oaks in the fields were all dead or dying. Many had had the ground beneath their canopies ploughed up, with fatal results for the trees' root systems and the complex ecology of fungi that feed and support them.

I reached the top of the hill and a gate into a meadow, and recognized an ancient place straight away. It was an odd shape, like a miniature green with funnels of hedged grassland leading off it in several directions, and with a maze of hedges and moats. The grass itself was grazed by cattle, and very uneven, with banks and hummocks and the line of an old earthwork running along one perimeter, close to a moated wood that was really still part of this same intriguing corner.

I had passed within two or three hundred yards of this place for years and never realized it was there.

Towards the middle was a moat-like pond around what may have once been an island but was now an inundated patch of reeds. The spinney was moated, and a variety of old pollard oaks and ashes presided over the hedges and two additional ponds at other corners of the meadow.

The lane issued from the far side of the little meadow and plunged steeply downhill in a grassy drift overhung by more old oaks. This, I have since discovered, has always been the favoured local tobogganing hill, drawing people from miles around, as good hills are hard to find in most of Suffolk.

Later, over an impromptu lunch with a local farmer friend, Dave Pratt, I discovered that this was indeed an interesting spot. It was a medieval farm and yard, and had been excavated a few years back by a local archaeologist, Ruth Downing. Dave said all the ponds around Ubbeston are on the tops of hills. The moated wood must have supplied coppice wood for the farm, and its moat would have helped keep out cattle and deer from grazing the young shoots.

As we sat in his kitchen, Dave spoke of the nature reserves near the coast where he rented the grazing for his cattle. He questioned some of the management of these wetlands. Why didn't the RSPB control predators – the foxes and crows that stole the eggs and chicks of the plovers and other waders that nested out there?

A good many of the local farmers round Laxfield, Hevening-ham, Ubbeston and Dennington were keen on conservation and retained their hedges and smaller fields. I found large numbers of hedgerow pollard oaks around there, all doing well.

I stand in the little pightle, admiring one particular perfectly spherical, ideally shaped tree, a pollard oak in the hedge, and another, a pollard ash on the edge of the wood, its roots sunk to its knees in the moat water. The tree against a dark grey sky with charcoal lines of rain cloud approaching.

9th January

A wild, windy night and a bright, clear windy day. I walk out along Cowpasture Lane and up the hill to the pollard hornbeam, definitely a trasmocho tree with its unusually wide bolling. On the way I stand leaning on the little wooden bridge over the stream at the ford, watching the running water. Then a long trudge into the wind to reach the badger sett, still very active and well trodden, with claw marks in the mud everywhere. The wood is creaking, and a sound like a squeaky hinge sings out where two birches are rubbing against each other. From the mud hill-fort of the badger sett, beaten paths radiate into the wood and out across a plank bridge into the weedy set-aside field beyond the wood. In the long shadows of the late white sun it is easy to make them out and to follow one over the field to a ditch crossing and all the way to a gap in the wire fence of the railway embankment, where the badgers scratch themselves against the wire and leave little clumps of their shaving-brush hair on the grass. I walk to the lane in the shadow and shelter of the tall embankment and scuttle home, glad of the shelter of the lane's hedges.

Dartmoor. Little waterspouts at the side of the road at Ashburton. Ferny, high banks, holly hedges and hazel, built up atop the stone walls, and gnarled weather-beaten beeches, the trunks crusted with lichen and quilted with moss. Sheep penned in small stone-walled fields. Clumps of John / Paul Nash beeches on the hilltops, leaning, brushed into shape by the wind like a woman's hair when she leans one way to shake it out and brush it. Trees all tend towards the east, brushed by the west wind and laid down. Crouching, flat-topped hedges – beech.

Swollen streams and rivers – the Beck and Brook. Hard to see which is snaking road and which river. Then up through a gate and across a cattle grid and you're on the moor. Three-foot pillars of granite, forming a hut circle beside the road. Low clumped gorse. Pony dung, sheep droppings, the great jagged Hound Tor. Clitters of stones and rocks.

Otters trotting, the swishing of fish. Wistman's Wood – a tangle of slender spidery tree trunks, hirsute with lichen.

Below Ashburton, the Dart careers down in straight cascades. You climb up to the moor through woods of tall spindly oak/ash/holly, ivy clambering up them all. Long houses hunker down into the hills/hollows, beauty in the undulations of their slated and thatched roofs, their eaves, their windows.

The great thing about walking is that it gives you complete licence to get into fancy dress and eat junk food.

At the lower Cherry Brook, near Manaton – a children's swimming hole and a rope in an oak bough and a rubber tyre. I swing out over the little river.

Walking back from the Devonport Leat, the bright lights of the Two Bridges Hotel suddenly visible. A fox bounds across the moor in the headlights and melts into the hedge.

It was wintertime on the northern flanks of Dartmoor, and I was following the River Teign along the Two Moors Way when I noticed a pair of mallards swimming against the stream, edging upstream close to the bank, deftly following the eddy current against the powerful main current of a river swollen with winter rain.

They seemed to personify a great deal about Dartmoor – about the determined spirit of resistance to hardship and difficulty. Everything has to contend with difficulties of one kind or another. The toughness that underlies the beauty gives it a specially enduring quality.

Dartmoor is both intensely liberating and a prison. Sam North's recent novel *The Lie of the Land* describes the sheer shackling grind of a working farm struggling to survive on the moor.

It is not a wilderness in the American sense – far from a trackless waste, it is full of the signs of human and animal life. People have swarmed all over this moor, and still do, in search of riches of one kind or another, or refuge, or recreation.

Everywhere are the signs of alchemy – the tinner's delvings into the body of the moor. Someone far back in the pre-Phoenician days had discovered that tin ore, cassiterite, will smelt into tin at about 1,100°C. The tinner's blowing houses were thatched and the thatch stripped and burnt every so often, to capture the particles of tin lodged there.

There is water everywhere on Dartmoor, tumbling in every direction. And it is by water that you may find your way in what is an otherwise trackless wilderness. It is one of the last great wild places in England, one of the fifty royal forests that still retains its integrity, one of the few places in England where you can stand alone and remote, and quite out of earshot of any road. The towns and villages that surround the moor are twinkling so far off you feel you're in a different time as well as place.

You take the familiar silhouette for granted in winter, but you would miss it if it wasn't there.

Fire: nothing gives me more comfort or more anxiety than fire.

Look up Cobbett on the laying of fires – talk about bread ovens and faggots of furze for bread-making.

The fireplace has been subsumed by the TV, pushed out of the nest as by a cuckoo. People now contemplate the TV, not the fire.

A fire only really comes into its own when it is genuinely needed – when the weather is so cold that you come in shivering, preferably red of nose, blue of cheek and perhaps white of toenail.

Our immediate ancestors bathed before the fire in slipper baths – hot water came from the copper. Life revolved around the fire and the kitchen range, and the coal cellar or wood-shed. Think what we miss when we press buttons or flick switches or adjust thermostats – a whole world of mystery and delight.

Fire is by no means silent; it crackles, wheezes, whistles. There are few sights more beautiful than wood smoke hovering over a copse in autumn/February, when the coppicers are at work.

At the party last night people talked about walking in the hills, or the countryside, but they always had to prefix 'walking' with 'dog'. As though walking were not a sufficient end in itself. Going walking is eccentric; going 'dog-walking' is a practical necessity, and the dog is perceived as a connection with nature, whereas in fact the opposite is true.

A dog cuts you off from much of the wildlife you might otherwise encounter by disturbing and alarming things. In the larger picture, dogs are a serious disturbance to, for example, ground-nesting birds and hares. They have successfully chased away both of these from our common over recent years, when there has been a rise in the population of the village and in particular of newcomers developing and building what were once farmyards and barns into new homes. Almost all of them appear to own dogs, in some cases as many as six, and many ignore the injunctions of the Suffolk Wildlife Trust to exercise their animals on a lead.

I keep uncovering more and more evidence for a Murphy's Law of publishing: that if a book is truly wonderful, it is certain to be out of print. Last week I tried to buy a copy of T. H. White's *The Goshawk* for a friend and found it unobtainable. This week I've been on the trail of Richard Jefferies's *Bevis*, also out of print, and number one million-something in the Amazon.com sales ratings. I eventually discovered twenty-nine copies available, all but one in America. Richard Jefferies deserves better than this, and he is getting it from Green Books with this essential collection of his later writings, at a time in his life when he had become more mature and thoughtful – his prose better than ever.

Yesterday, I began cutting and reshaping the overgrown ash arch from one end. I laid the branches, half cutting through them at an angle, then bending them down as I stood on the ladder or step-ladder, and weaving them into the arch to hold them down, or securing them with string.

Later, at dusk, I went out and planted a few maples and hawthorns on the common outside the house by the big willow. I bought them from Eddie Krutysza this morning in Metfield, and I bought a red-flowering may tree too, and planted it in the corner of the garden.

Something pale in the darkness caught my eye, a pale ghost gliding silently about the common – a barn owl hunting six feet above the grass, dropping almost petulantly now and again, only to rise empty-clawed almost on the instant.

I kept on digging and planting, digging and planting, well into darkness until I could see nothing.

The barn owl was there again this afternoon about three o'clock, its wingspan huge and its lightness palpable in its floating mode of flight. I know how frail and fragile owls really are when you lift them, and worry each time a car or lorry comes belting far too fast along the common. The owl likes to fly along the verge, perilously close to the traffic, with no apparent fears for its safety.

I worked on the ash arch for three and a half hours yesterday afternoon. It feels like a chess game, or giant pick-a-stick, circling the arch, trying to decide which branch to bend next, and in which direction.

The branches of the ash arch are now laid like a hedge and

folded into each other, ready to bud and thrust into new life in spring as soon as the sap rushes back up the trees' veins and seeps through the hinges of grisly bent wood that connect trunk and bent bough.

I love the creasing and wrinkling of the tree's skin at the points where branches have been bent over and then healed, like the bending of an elephant's trunk. Woodmen call these 'elbows', and I have often found, in Welsh or Cumbrian hedges especially, that the laid branches of hazel or ash will pleach themselves together, two or three different trees fusing into one in a series of swollen, gnarled elbows.

23rd January

The first wood pigeon cooing in a tree by the house. I open the curtain and there is a squirrel. We all know how a squirrel moves, yet my heart leaps at the sight of its sudden rushes in the grass around the base of the mulberry, seeking out peanuts that have dropped out of my improvised feeder – a recycled orange-bag from the supermarket filled with peanuts. His sleekness and perfect fur; waves of fur as he moves. Then he suddenly takes fright as he makes sense of my shape at the window desk, and runs off.

Coppicing is like making waves. You cut down a wave of vegetation, then another comes a few years later. Wave upon wave, making a wood's history, and evident in the rippling waves of the annual rings.

Music is like the decorative, symphonic possibilities of a

wood: endless combinations of notes or twigs, leaves and wind, branch shapes against the sky.

'The lost score of a jig' – fighting back beyond the oblivion of last night's sleep to the thought I was too sleepy to write down.

Richard [Mabey] and I talked about the upsurge of religion in America. Why is this? Perhaps because of a need for history, a hunger for the history they lack. The bible supplies a kind of instant history for them. Its simple presence in their homes gives them a rooted feeling in history.

Others have turned to the land for their sense of history: to nature and the millennia of evolutionary and geological history. These are the deep ecologists.

We talked about America and I said I would like to go in search of Robert Frost land – the land I inhabited through my adolescence reading Frost, the New England of 'The Road Not Taken' – and I said I hoped there wouldn't be an interpretation board at the bisection of the two roads – a sign pointing at 'The Road Not Taken'.

We talked about interpretation in Tasmania and America – how there are different *zones* or *grades* of land – National Park, Nature Reserve and, in America, State Forest, National Nature Reserve, National Park, etc.

In Tasmania, when I followed certain 'walking tracks', I would reach some wild eminence and encounter a sort of viewing platform with a wooden banister rail and a plaque inscribed with a line or two of a poem telling you what to think and feel, and which way to look.

I talked about Colin Ward's new book, and his idea that houses should *not* be built fast, on seven-month schedules, but organically, by slow accretions, over many years of habitation and out of the natural needs and requirements that arise.

Richard told me about a woodworker who made something out of a piece of the Selborne yew. He said yew cracked too much to turn. I went and fetched Matt Marchbank's beautiful yew bowl, turned a few Christmases ago, to show him. 'Must have been a young tree,' he said.

24th January
In the early sunshine, I strip to the waist, sit outside on the kitchen doorstep before a mirror propped up in a cane chair and cut my hair. It feels good, even rejuvenating, to strip off the professor-like abundance of locks and to feel the sun on my skin.

25th January
I am at Mellis in drenching fine rain with a deep grey pall of sky, a wide skirt of it overhanging the common.

Aconites, a little yellow clump by the moat, are just beginning to come up. I scare two mallard drakes parked up, as it ' were, on the moat. The moat is a kind of holding bay for drakes, where they hang about waiting for the rare moments of sudden sexual frenzy when a duck appears and there's a gang-bang. Mallards seem incapable of ordinary, fonder bird-love. With them, it has to be a violent chase, wild pursuit, followed by an unceremonious ducking of the object of desire and a gang-bang, with a lot of ruffian quacking.

The tower room. Towers have a reputation as refuges for writers. Yeats had one at Thoor Ballylee, Montaigne had one in Bordeaux, and Keats and Cyril Connolly were always imagining them. There was a tower at the gamekeeper's cottage near Beccles where my London flatmates and I used to escape at weekends in the 1960s. You couldn't reach it from the house, but had to go in from the garden and up a spiral staircase to a little upstairs room with bare walls and just a table and chair. You sat looking out into the woods, or stared out of the window, sharpened pencils, etc., and wrote. Or at least that was the idea.

Previous occupants of the table had made contributions to an informal anthology of graffiti, variously inspiring or depressing. 'Getting and spending, we lay waste our lives.' And the whole of Robert Graves's poem about the young bird-catcher on his way through the woods. Other contributions included the lines from Yeats about 'marriage with a fool', and an original couple of lines by Tony Barrell about Magritte and kittiwakes.

Water had to be pumped out of a well, and an old Lister

petrol engine inside a box in the garden had to be hand-cranked. The crank had a nasty habit of kicking back or running away with you, and bandaged wrists were one of the regular features of life at the cottage. Bandaged ankles were another, thanks to the deep ruts everywhere. The place was sequestered in the woods far from any public road and was generally reached by train from London to Beccles, where we kept an Austin Champ, a kind of four-miles-to-the-gallon military jeep, in the car park. A sign of the times was that we always left the keys in the ignition. You drove as far as the Little David petrol station at Stockton, then turned off along a muddy track across the fields and through the woods.

We seemed to spend a great deal of our time servicing the house. The rule was that you saved up and collected at least as much firewood as you burnt. There was no electricity, so fires, candles and paraffin were all the more vital. There was a stove in the kitchen over which we spent much time huddled. It took ages to get into its stride and was usually just about going nicely when it was time to leave.

There was always the pub, of course: the Wherry at Geldeston was not far away. There were beds everywhere, upstairs and down, and several layers of the rags and carpets you could pick up for next to nothing at auctions (bare feet being one of the orders of the day).

Star favourites in the paperback library under the stairs were the novels of Geoffrey Household, *Rogue Male* in particular. Barrell derived the verb 'to quive' from this book (Major Quive-Smith is the gentlemanly villain of the piece) to describe wriggling along a leafy ditch bottom, flat on your chest in pursuit of, or flight from, whatever or whoever you didn't want to see you. The whole of *Rogue Male* may be said to be one long quive from beginning to end. Barrell and I used to write blurbs for Oliver Caldecott, then the Penguin fiction editor

(I did *Rogue Male, A Rough Shoot* and *Watcher in the Shadows*).

We wore corduroy in those days: Barrell wore navy, Chapman wore black, I wore dark brown. I also went in for brown herringbone tweed jackets or overcoats. The jacket was very expensive, bought from Jaeger after working with Ken Russell, who wore the full works: brown herringbone trousers, jacket and matching cap. I couldn't even afford the jacket, but bought one anyway.

I now realize that all these English country-gentleman outfits were designed to make you look as much like a ploughed field as possible.

The modest scale of the cottage, the large number of us and the informal proximity of beds and copious intoxicants created a dormitory atmosphere, and there was much talking after lights-out. Barrell invented an organic breakfast cereal to be called 'Dobbin'. I think it was dried cow-pats, flaked and mixed with a few raisins. Now and again there were mushrooms. And in that era there were still plenty of authentic Suffolk bumpkins to be met, or seen stumping about Beccles.

Stockton Wood was well supplied with pheasants, and we all learnt to appreciate them as individual characters. Our affection for them probably led to their downfall, by making them far too trusting. The boy at the Little David garage kept tame magpies and jays in an aviary. They were very clever, and no doubt well fed, but we felt sorry for them all the same. There were good second-hand bookshops all over Suffolk then, and we rarely returned to London empty-handed.

One of our main preoccupations was photography. Barrell, in particular, took it very seriously and toted a Pentax or a Nikon around the woods and hedgerows. We made weekly expeditions to Bungay, to the fish café for lunch and some covert portraiture with the telephoto lens. Elizabeth Smart lived a few miles outside Bungay, deep in the Flixton estate at the end of a very long lane in a place called 'The Dell'. And that is exactly what it was: a cottage built on the site of what once was a sand quarry. Elizabeth had made a beautiful garden that shaded off into the wilderness of the surrounding thickets and woodland. It was full of ramshackle sheds and summer-houses where visitors could sleep, carpets slung over the earth floor. There was even the old estate gas house with boiler and brick chimney, home of the bar whenever Elizabeth had one of her parties.

I turned up there once with a friend one evening, long before there were mobile phones. We had been canoeing down the River Waveney and had beached our craft close by, when a sudden thunderstorm caught us. We found Elizabeth and George Barker in the full swing of a wake for their late friend Patrick Kavanagh, and joined them for an evening of strenuous whiskey-drinking.

I missed my friends as I missed my trees when I was away in Australia. I missed Ronnie and preferred to think of him at home in Suffolk like an oak.

There are many of us for whom the shed is a natural habitat. Mine is full of woodworking tools: a classic Myford ML8

lathe, band-saw, circular-saw and various drills, Skil-saws, planes. A whole wall of screwdrivers, chisels and gauges, and little drawers full of screws and fixings. Shelves of varnish, oils, stains and paints, and more drawers with drill bits, seeds, cramps, vices, an adze and several wedges for splitting wood. Hand-saws, jigsaws.

The big workbench once belonged to the communal farm Middleton Murry founded at Thelnetham when he lived there. It is tough and scarred, pitted and ingrained with the marks and grime of eighty years of hard work.

There is other furniture too, of a kind: an old table with drawers where all the chucks and spindles for the lathe live, with the long-handled chisels and gauges in a rack above it, and the electric grinder to one side for sharpening them. On the wall beside the chisels is a photograph torn from a newspaper of the woodworker David Pye, and his obituary. DP was the great champion of diversity, in his own work, and in all made things, as the tonic our souls require.

The shed is lit by a collection of theatrical floodlights slung from the ceiling beams, and a pair of anglepoise lamps that can be focused on the lathe.

A variety of hunks of oak, cherry, sycamore, ash, hazel, hornbeam and walnut sit about in various corners or help weigh down the lathe and other electrical machinery. Stabilizing the lathe is crucial to woodturning. This is the reason woodturners often covet the big old machines like the Harrison Graduate, a bowl-turning lathe whose sheer weight in steel will ensure that it never moves or so much as vibrates. The slightest vibration can cause the chisel to jump on the spinning wood and split or tear into it.

Books are like seeds: they come to life when you read them, and grow spines and leaves. I need trees around me as I need books around me, so building bookshelves is something like planting trees.

Strong winds rattling the willow tops against each other. Constant rasping and clicking of twigs – rain driving across the common. I go out to prune the lavatera and the buddleia, cutting it back hard. Then I set to work pollarding the small willow by the gate. It has fourteen poles about twenty feet long, and I cut nine of them by hand, stripping off the side shoots with the billhook and stacking the twigs and small branches on the dead hedge along the north-western boundary of this garden. I stack the poles against the big crack willow with the ash poles Rufus [Deakin, Roger's son] and I cut down before Christmas.

I finish work at dark, and a moon comes up, pale and windswept. The cats can't wait to come in the house and curl up straight away in their favourite places, Millie behind the Aga, Alf on a sofa.

A big full moon low in the sky at 7 a.m., windy, clear, puddles all the way up the common, moon sitting on the horizon, rooks flying and tumbling west with the wind. Pigeons too, all birds have come out to play in the seductive wind.

February

The squirrel is the English cosimo, running along in the trees, quite as happy diving headlong down a slender tree trunk as climbing up it. They remind me of the Big Brother system of brass cylinders that used to shoot along a system of pneumatic tubes held aloft on the ceilings of Harrods, where I once worked in the blanket-packing department.

3rd February

Filming a pilot for Channel 4 all day with Mike [Dibb]. We begin with pollards: the two willows by the moat and the pollard cherry woven into a basket, and the little oak tree by the doorway of the green woodshed.

Then we move on to the coppiced hazel, and the ash bower, and I mention David Nash and how this is the beginning of the Gothic arch in architecture. Then we look at the ash spiral, and the relation of wood to water, and the pleasure of seeing the architecture of trees in winter, when they are bare of leaves.

After lunch, we move on to the common and I talk about the big oak tree, free-standing, free-growing and wild because no forester has interfered with it or lopped its branches to create a straighter trunk with fewer knots. Instead, this oak has done exactly as it pleases, and attained an entirely natural shape, not having been jostled for space and light by other trees, as a woodland oak would be. It has grown under optimum conditions, in good soil undisturbed by the plough, manured by generations of cows congregating beneath it for shade, with all its vital mycorhizal fungi undisturbed and functioning. A profoundly contented and healthy tree.

I talk about the architecture of a tree, about its essential cone shape, with the branches cantilevered from the central tower of the trunk, tubular structures being the strongest. I stand beneath the branches and say there are thirty-five of them, and that their combined weight must be several tons. I love the horizontality of oak. Of all trees, it has the strength to float its outstretched branches out at ninety degrees to the trunk. These horizontal branches exert enormous forces at the cantilevered joint, which must be immensely strong. That is why the joint pieces are so sought after by carpenters and shipwrights. They are the 'knees' of ships, binding the ribbed frame together, joining the horizontal keel to the upright stern and bow.

By contrast with the old aspen that stands beside it on the common, the oak has retained all of its thirty-five branches. The aspen has only five left, the rest having been broken off by the wind. This tells you why oak is so greatly valued in this country.

Then we move inside and film a fire-lighting sequence in the main fireplace, talking about the architecture of fire, and the fact that most people in this world cook and warm themselves with wood as their fuel. Finally, something on David Nash and his work, and on the structure of the house itself: a skeleton house, not a 'crustacean' house, as Le Corbusier put it.

There are 243 beams in this house, proportions natural, set by the size of trees and their girth.

5th February

I spent from 3 p.m. until the light ran out at 5.30 p.m. making a cut-and-warp column for Terence [Blacker]'s birthday out of a length of green cherry log. It was three feet tall and I had put in thirty saw cuts – a total of 120 if you count each cut as being four, from each side. It is punishing work, and the sweat flowed freely. I worked at my improvised wooden anvil of oak and willow logs, big cross-sections of tree trunk heavy enough to take a firm hold of the workpiece. First I squared off the four sides of bark to make a square-sided column that tapered a little towards the top.

Making a cut-and-warp column is a good example of what David Pye calls 'the workmanship of risk'. At any moment things could go wrong. Tip the whizzing blade of the chainsaw an inch too far into the centre, and you could undo all your painstaking work by cutting short the column. You walk a tightrope from beginning to end of what feels more and more like a performance as you go on, your glasses steam up in the cold air, you enter a trance of concentration and the sweat runs down your back and springs itchily into your scalp inside the safety helmet, behind the medieval gauze visor, and streams down your forehead. Your eyes water in the frosty air.

After the first few incisions, you get into a rhythm and instinctively feel how deep to plunge the saw blade into the wood. By making a series of circular incisions no more than a quarter of an inch apart, you are left with a series of wooden leaves suspended, cantilevered on a slender central column of continuous heart wood. The bar of your chainsaw is three eighths of an inch thick, so with each cut you are removing as much wood as you leave standing in the sculpture, and letting a new element, air, into the wood. Thus you begin to open the tree to the air and allow the sap to evaporate, breathing it in yourself as you do so.

With each new incision, the sculpture becomes more fragile and the potential minor disaster if you were to make a mistake that much greater. As the time goes by and the piece grows more interesting, your investment in it becomes that much greater.

At last you make the final cut, and carry the sculpture into the house for the first time, cradling it in your arms like a baby.

You set it down on a table and scrutinize it from every angle, from close up and from the other side of the room. It feels good. You run a hot bath and sink into it, and lie soaking your tired limbs for a long time.

7th February
A walk up Cowpasture Lane with Jan Stevenson and Richard. The first mistle thrush singing in the garden. We find a stinking hellebore in the far end of the lane near the railway. Form a Cowpasture Lane Society and buy the lane?

8th February
The moat on Mellis Common. I believe its ecology goes something like this. It has always nearly run dry during autumn and early winter, filling with water in spring, but well drained enough not to fill very deep. For much of the year water lies over much of its length to a depth of six inches to a foot, no more, over a bed of twigs and leaves falling from the dense spinney and hedge that overhang it. This seems to be an ideal home to the ten-spined stickleback, and I have noticed over many years that a phenomenon long known and reported from the Lincolnshire fens occurs here: swarming shoals of the little fish, feasting carnivorously on the many insects and grubs that fall from the trees, and on the daphnia and other tiny organisms in the water. Sometimes you see the water boiling with them.

Kingfishers have always frequented these moats, hunting the sticklebacks along them. The shallower the water becomes as it drains, the easier prey the sticklebacks are.

Eventually, around August and September, there is so little water left in the moats that it concentrates in smaller, shallow pools that can seem to boil with the massed sticklebacks crowding into them. I have become convinced of the importance of shallow water to the kingfishers and sticklebacks. As the water grows deeper, the sticklebacks cease to thrive. They are pond fish, and they seem to be adapted for life in the shallows.

Kingfishers are so much a part of the life of Mellis Common along these moats and ponds that when the barn fronting the pond and common moat to the west of Cowpasture Farm was converted into a house ten or fifteen years ago, its developer christened it 'Kingfisher Barn'.

However, the development interfered with the traditional flow and level of the water draining through the system of ponds and moats around Mellis Common. First, the fine old brick-arched bridge that carried a cart track into the Cow-pasture barns, and over which hundreds of cows went in and out to the milking sheds for hundreds of years, was demolished. The pipe installed as a substitute for the open arch of the original bridge does not seem to be adequate to take the volume of water running along the moat system. That the water should be continually flowing is, of course, vital to maintaining oxygen levels and diminishing the adverse effects of eutrophication.

The pipe draining water from the Cowpasture Farm pond has also been relaid at a much higher level, thus effectively damming the pond, raising the level all the way back to Cowpasture Lane, and radically altering the nature of the system of moats and ponds as habitat for a chain of plants and animals that traditionally includes ten-spined sticklebacks and kingfishers as a notable component, as well as toads, frogs and newts, some of which also value shallows as breeding grounds. The recent introduction of larger fish, notably roach and rudd, will also be affecting the ability of frogs, toads and newts to breed successfully in the ponds, while they themselves will be too big to be of much interest to kingfishers.

They do, however, attract herons, especially by night and in the very early hours of the morning.

The water level has risen some two or three feet.

Squirrels. The way they nosedive down trees or swing, up-ended, on the peanut dispenser is like a leaden clock pendulum.

The way they dive down trees, the way they know how to fall from one tree to another – a delicate, twitching flag of fur. Falling like a yellow duster dropped from an upstairs window.

I have built a sort of wooden anvil on a level concrete pad where I store timber, work at my sculptures and split logs. It is a makeshift arrangement of large willow, oak and ash logs, cross-sections of tree trunks laid flat, notched and stepped up or down like Lego depending on the level at which I want to labour with my chainsaw. They are scarred with the criss-cross signature of the saw blade, which they cannot harm.

Labouring amongst them the other day, and in the full flow of artistic creation, I kicked two or three logs to clear some floor space and uncovered a huddle of froglets like a heap of small change hunkered down and cowering in the damp sawdust beneath the logs. Regretting my carelessness, I bent down to move the creatures under cover and realized I had wounded one of them. Blood oozed from a wound on its side as it dragged itself out of sight under some bark. I felt nasty, guilty and brutal all night and next day. Under another log was a newt, and I was reminded of the secret lives that go on all around here all the time.

9th February

The decline of the Church of England is a specially dangerous thing in rural areas. It means the vicars keep on changing every few years because there aren't enough of them to go round, and anyway the church no longer attracts the high quality of minds it once did. To make matters worse, each vicar has to look after a 'group' of parishes, so lacks the local knowledge and intimacy with the natural surroundings he or she would need to carry authority when pronouncing on conservation, questions of.

In earlier times a Gilbert White or a Parson Woodforde would have been quick to spot anything amiss with nature in the parish and to speak forthrightly about it to any wrongdoers. Not any more. Worse still, you have vicars who come in and cut down cedar trees in churchyards, or yews.

12th February

Walking along Cowpasture Lane and Howe Lane to Thornham Parva. The trees are all wrong in Howe Lane near Thornham Parva Church. They exhibit all the classic ills of tree-planting. Whoever did it simply had not the faintest idea what they were doing. Cherries and walnuts are interspersed with pathetic little hawthorns in tight double rows in ugly white plastic tubes. Where is all that plastic supposed to end up? Just a few field maples too – but the whole lot of them bred in a greenhouse in Holland from original progeny in Romania or somewhere far off. Similarly, those hawthorns you see in full blossom in mid March on the motorway come from further south and think its spring in their plant-clocks.

They've planted walnuts inches away from hawthorns, and they hate competition. And they've planted them no more than nine or ten feet apart when they need to be spaced thirty or thirty-five feet, so they have space to develop their huge crowns. The walnut has the biggest canopy of any English tree.

The history of the countryside is far more a history of skulduggery of one kind or another than has generally been recognized. Written records are of only moderate usefulness in delivering up the past: most of the real action was never recorded because it took place on the wrong side of the law.

The shaping of so many of the old pollards along Cowpasture Lane would probably be a very gradual, mostly surreptitious process, involving the covert removal of odd branches, possibly by night or very early morning: a kind of illicit pruning over many hundreds of years.

People are still helping themselves to quite valuable hunks of common land right under the noses of the entire village where I live in Suffolk. When I arrived here in 1970, a farmer was helping himself quite openly to the two and half acres occupied by an ancient droving road that may well have been there for 4,000 years. He bulldozed and uprooted the hedges and copse trees, and dynamited the more spectacular of the oaks. It was a major piece of work, and he was assisted with a grant from the helpful Ministry of Agriculture.

The removal of thousands of miles of old hedgerows was an act of breathtaking skulduggery in itself. In what other area of work except agriculture could people get away with such obvious vandalism?

Lanes were removed or moved, footpaths rerouted, maps redrawn by little mafias of landowners up and down the country. In our own parish, the farmers got together in 1969/70 to redraw the parish map to their own convenience, downgrading byways to footpaths at the stroke of a pen, with no accountability to anyone at all.

13th February
A sunny, cold but almost springish day. I can't resist pottering outside, re-erecting the rose on props of ash and hazel, burrowing away the ash cuttings in piles from under the ash arch. Then I cut some firewood with a bow-saw at the bench and go for a bike ride.

The first thing the cats did today was rush about all over the garden and race up all the trees as high as they could go. Next they went hunting on the common, and Millie soon caught a mouse that she paralysed, taunted and then ate on the brick terrace with an audible crunching of bones.

Yesterday I went swimming – only thirty lengths – but I immediately felt miles better. The exercise, and a few final moments in the sauna, energized me for the rest of the day, and I slept much better too.

Tonight, the skies are clear and the temperature is dropping sharply. There will be a frost. I'm glad I fixed the chimney flashing earlier in the week.

I spent a lot of time today mooning about my hedges, inspecting sheds and their cobwebby contents, and contemplating how I would lay the hedge of the railway wood.

Cutting up firewood, I came across a stem of elm wonderfully inlaid with the workings of a beetle. An English scribbly bark.

The ash arch looks its best in the early morning frost, which highlights and etches out its form in white.

A soft, grey morning, cold but neither windy nor frosty. Green-finches, chaffinches, robins all over the garden, queuing to eat peanuts from the feeder. I'm thinking of Kyrgyzstan and Osh: the hotel with its threadbare rugs and breakfast of hot bread and honey brought in to me at seven, set down on a low table walled in by old sofas, worn and dusty. Everything dusty, and the bathroom barely working. Cold water, a dribbling shower.

Starlings now appear singly, not in the flocks I remember in Mellis. No sparrows, just chaffinches, blue tits, great tits, long-tailed tits and the jester in the pack, the great spotted woodpecker. A dunnock picking up the crumbs beneath, hesitant and watchful.

14th February

A walk down the lane with Andrew [Sanders] in a bitter cold north wind to Thornham Wood, the badger sett, and a circuit of some of the wood. Two or three squirrels' dreys in oaks up the lane, amazingly complex pollard oaks. A crow nose-dived into the field. Meadows and grassy rides horribly ploughed by 4WD tracks. A recent and nasty development – urban habit of treating every meadow as a car park. Saw two hares only. Used to be dozens of them. Saw no deer at all. All shot, I suspect.

15th February

Saturday morning I wake up in London and walk over to the Festival Hall after a hearty bacon and mushroom breakfast. Over Waterloo Bridge, and see a long queue of people eddying and dropping down the narrow well of stairs to the Embankment below like water going down a bath plug.

Amazing forest of placards on pine sticks provided by the *Mirror*. I found myself marching behind banners I couldn't read held by a bunch of women, with one reading, as I later discovered after being photographed by the press, 'Cunt-lovers Against the War'.

There were quite a few dogs on leads, 'Dogs of War', as one placard called them, and several poodles, including one led by a priest in full cassock with a banner behind it that read 'Poodle, Bite your Master's Leg'.

There were also several beautifully made huge swans, which flapped their diaphanous wings and seemed to fly above the crowd, a striking image in the park. Mike [Hodges] and I spoke up for the daffodils in Hyde Park that were getting trodden down and crushed, and a man climbed up into a plane tree in St James's Park to watch the march.

There were placards like 'Pagan Queers for Peace' and 'Cold? Wrap Yourself Up in a Woolly Liberal'.

Richard discovered long-lost friends like the Berkhamsted CND and the Woodcraft Folk.

Mike, Sarah Martin and Carol [Law] escaped from the park, meeting Caroline Soper and Hanif Kureishi on the way, picked up a free bottle or two of Mecca Cola, and squeezed through a narrow iron gateway with thousands of others to reach Marble Arch and the warmth of a café, then adjourned later to Cigala for a dinner of Caldeirada and rabbit paella, washed down with several bottles of an excellent Ribera del Duero wine called Martin Berdugo. Sarah Martin says she knows of a cork oak forest, where black pigs graze in the woods in the west of Andalusia near Murcia; and the hotel is owned by some people called Chesterton.

Drove home at 1 a.m., arriving at Mellis at 3 a.m., e-mails to Australia (big 500,000 march in Sydney), bed at 4 a.m.

16th February
Yesterday was a beautiful clear, sunny, cold, February day and I went walking in the Eye Town Moor. Dark, peaty earth and tracks soft and springy through the damp fen; I cross a wooden sleeper bridge over a brook laced with fool's watercress. The path weaves through the pale slender trunks of

ash trees I helped to plant fifteen years ago, now twenty feet high. This is a partly planted wood that has evolved in a random way through the imagination of an artist, Ben Platts-Mills.

There's a circle of tall ashes, planted two feet apart, entered through an arch formed by two branches bent over and pleached together. Then you wander past a pond with a mound beside it and a lover's bench with a pair of heart-shaped seat backs, and just beyond it you catch sight of a living woodhenge of stubby pollarded willows of different colours, their pollard heads like the hedgehog heads of comic characters from the *Beano*, or bog brushes (mop-headed).

There are the ruined remains of hippie-ish structures like a willow wigwam plaited together.

18th February
I had to fiddle about putting the car on the battery charger, then went up the field to rummage about in one of my sheds looking for an architrave. I love it in the shed. Half the tin roof has rusted through and caved in, but, instead of mending it, which would have meant cutting down some brambles to get round the back, I simply moved all the wooden architraves and mouldings into another part of the shed away from the drips.

The whole floor of the shed is under attack from the rabbits whose warren it is, so all the contents are constantly subsiding into the earth. It is a shed with subsidence.

I tiptoed my way in, past a couple of big sash windows from

a skip and a fine semicircular stained-glass window, and eased along to the far end. A legless Windsor smoker's bow chair: a lovely thing but in need of a set of legs. Another project for my nineties.

Removing several sections of stove pipe, I came across the canvas bed that would have been used to convey the grain and chaff to the threshing drum. I moved this and uncovered the pile of architraves and mouldings. All beautiful but all too short, and not a single one matching. I never knew it was possible to plane wood in so many different ways.

None of the pieces was right. A man called David Bill at Shepperton Studios had given them to me years ago, leftovers from commercial sets. Mock-dado rails. Spoof Edwardiana. And now here they were, a palace for spiders, a dust museum, a nuisance for the rabbits. In the end I drove to Diss and bought a new architrave from Jewson's.

Bright sunshine and cold at Mellis. Snipe drumming on the common in the big pond hollow on the way to Stonebridge.

I watch hundreds of fieldfares and starlings feeding on the molehills on the top common.

A walk in Burgate Wood with Robert Macfarlane. We try to work out the right word for what a pheasant call is – a squawk? Not enough. With grouse it is a 'crick' or 'cricking'. We climb into the high seat of a gamekeeper's deep-shooting vantage point at the crossroads of four rides and survey the autumn wood – the old coppice and pollard stems.

Rob spoke of Spitfire Books, publishing ripping tales for men in the spirit of a *Rover* comic or the *Eagle*. Also of Geoffrey Hill, writing on the countryside, and Ruskin leading his students off to dig a road outside Oxford to learn about hard work as the prerequisite of clear thinking. Same goes for Morris – obsessed with working *with the hands*, with *crafting* and *shaping* things.

We agreed to:

(1) Go together in search of the *Rogue Male* lane and hideout in Dorset.
(2) Go hiking in the Peak District and look for the white mountain hare.
(3) Have dinner in Emmanuel and drink port and look at the enormous plane trees in the gardens, etc.

Rob spoke of the need to find a new language to write about, say, wood. We both had written poems as a way into the work. I wrote *Waterlog* poems to limber up – my Chatham Docks poem, and my wheelbarrow poem. And Robert wrote his personal climbing experiences as poems before he wrote them as prose. I said Arthur Miller did this with his plays. Hence the very particular stage directions, as at the end of *The Crucible*: 'He touches her cheek, they both laugh, etc.' But also there is a preoccupation with shaping things – Miller had his workshop and furniture-making, and his barn-building and tree-planting.

20th February

I stand inside the kitchen doorway and watch sheets of rain blowing right to left across the field. Overnight the curtains I had washed by hand in the bath blew down off the washing line and had to be washed again.

An e-mail from Rufus in Ecuador after a 22-hour journey by bus from Lima. He speaks of a 'three-foot machete' he has bought in Peru. Andrew came to lunch, and I tried to clear up the appallingly cluttered kitchen. Everything covered in dust.

9.00 a.m. drive to Norwich to meet Jayne for a swim at UEA – superb feeling at last, gliding up and down in the green-blue water. Special sides which swallow the waves before they can ricochet. Monsieur Hulot effect on Jayne and me as we try to get past all the automatic barriers and gates with our entrance cards. (Great feeling of suppleness and fitness glow afterwards – all day.) A good day – lots of energy released.

21st February

I woke at 7.30 to snow. Snow sugaring the trees, snow three inches deep. The birds are busy feeding in the peanut tree, the only tree to bear fruit in February: pendulous cylinders of peanuts.

Blackbird, robin, sparrow, coal tit, greenfinch, chaffinch, blue tit, sparrow, great tit (more occasional), long-tailed tits, great spotted woodpecker, pheasant (cock) circling beneath, pecking up the peanut crumbs from the upper table. Mallards sliding under the hedges on the far side of the moat.

At 8.45 snow suddenly begins falling from the trees. When it snows, half the snowflakes seem to float upwards, not down.

It is starting to snow hard, a flurry and a confusion of big snowflakes, and the cock pheasant circling under the peanut tree.

Where there's a tree stump, an upturned bucket, a flower-pot, a watering can, snow settles on top and builds up like the crust on a loaf as it rises out of the baking tin, so everywhere you look in the vegetable garden you see appetizing white loaves.

Now here's Alfie, my black tom cat, all speckled with snow, and the snowflakes aren't melting on his coat at all – a sign of how well insulated he is inside his coat of fur.

My tame cock pheasant looks at his best in the snow. It shows off his tropical colours, the warm russets of his breast and his scarlet face, the park-bench green of his neck, and the sweep of his tail like a rudder in the snow.

Now it's snowing really hard – pixels of snow against the deep purple and crimson-browns of the sallows out on the common. You realize where Christo got the ideas for his sculptures when you see snow wrapping everything in white, softening all the outlines. It transforms things. Suddenly I have a snow car, with snow doors, a snow boot and a snow bonnet and windscreen.

We built a snowman here once, facing south beside the moat, and when the sun came out it softened one side of him and caused him to lean over backwards like an acrobat somersaulting. A somersaulting snowman. Winter-saulting.

There was a full-grown fox with big pads here, and he knew exactly where he was going: due east. Ah, but here he paused, saw something, went due north for a couple of yards, then resumed his course to the east. The tracks disappear into the hedge. In summer the foxes run along in the ditches, but it's too wet for that now.

Now here's a green woodpecker feeding like a blackbird under the mulberry tree, pecking about for tiny grubs in the grass. The velvet-green of its breast and the crimson lake of its nape are perfectly complementary; except they are never simple colours but a subtle, complex blend of many.

The cock chaffinches are a shifty lot; they hang around the bird-feeder, surreptitiously advance up the hazel poles to pole position at the top, sing a little song of 'King of the Castle', then wait for a hen bird to come to feed, and swoop on her.

22nd February
Another frosty, light-snowy night and a brilliant sunny morning.

When the sun comes out and shines on the molehills, you

can imagine them as a mountain range. The molehills on the common – who says we live in a flat county? Who says the common has never been ploughed? The moles plough it.

What you need to write is energy, sexual potency and solitude. Swimming gave me plenty of all three, stimulating the hormones as it sharpened up the stamina, and isolating me with one of the great universal elements.

Walking up Stonebridge Lane, I wonder about its true width – surely greater than this strip of patchy grass left unploughed?

There's a myth in this country that the professionals are better at things than the amateurs: that they know more, and get things right. I believe the opposite to be true. At any rate there is far too great a gulf between the two worlds of the amateur and the professional.

Take country history and archaeology. The County Definitive Maps people, researching away in the Records Office, looking for documentary evidence of rights of way and so on, are unaware of the existence of Norman Scarfe and the Suffolk Archaeological Society – they live in a separate, sealed world.

Last night, in the Bury St Edmunds Tesco car park, a single song thrush singing clearly, perched six or seven feet up in a low tree – some ornamental tree amongst the cotoneaster shrubbery beside the River Lark. It sang in the full glare of an orange sodium lamp and hardly faltered when I approached within ten feet of it.

I mentioned it excitedly to the Indian doorman. 'I don't

know about birds – only parrots,' he said. The woman inside at the tobacco counter knew about the bird. 'It's been singing for a week or so now,' she said.

My contention is that in every weed, bramble and migrating bird, the wilderness asserts itself, so when Hopkins wrote 'Long live the weeds and the wilderness yet' at the end of 'Inversnaid', he was articulating the essential drive of nature towards the re-establishment of the wilderness. Growing up immediately after the war, I witnessed how quickly and rampantly wilderness took over the bomb sites, covering them in fireweed, brambles and buddleia.

When pheasants are on display, they drop their wings slightly, like a woman with a bun letting her hair down a little, but not completely. The frock-coat effect is incredibly elegant. The drooping wing feathers like a low bow.

24th February

Lunch with Vicky [Minet] and Sally [Mantoudis] and a walk in Vicky's wood, Slough Grove, afterwards. Lots of underscrub of mossy elder and overgrown hazel. Slender ash, and cherry, and some poplar. The ash was once coppiced, now very tall and waving in the wind. Rooks beginning to think of nesting. Chas, a friend, has coppiced and cleared an area of wood and protected the hazel stools with big domes of woven sticks.

Shoots are coming through after just one year. Bluebells everywhere, and we walk down rides Vicky keeps open by cutting with a tractor or topper once a year. Two ashes have toppled, crashing down and snapping six feet off the ground.

25th February

Fay Godwin on Ted Hughes's death. 'I still cannot believe he has been felled.' Poets as trees – see Keats, and Kim Taplin's essay on Keats.

Poaching is a symptom of poverty. People have to need a rabbit or a pheasant and need it enough to pluck or skin it and gut it too, and hang it a few days in the shed.

Nowadays you would simply wander into the supermarket and nick something more portable.

Pheasants, not rabbits, have more than a token market value now. Pheasant-poaching stopped when the gamekeeper began feeding the birds a fungicide or pesticide in the food to stop them catching some kind of poultry disease. Deer-poaching used to be profitable. 'All the poachers came from Wood Green for some reason,' a Diss police sergeant told me; you could get £500 for a red deer in a London hotel. Then came Chernobyl and the hotels stopped buying. Wild deer ingest far more radioactivity than any other animal and high concentrations build up in their bodies.

My police informant used to work in Hertfordshire around Bishop's Stortford, and the gangs would come out from Wood Green and work the woods. Rifles were more strictly controlled than shotguns, and so carried higher penalties if found on a poacher's person. Instead, the poachers converted shotguns into rifles like this: they undid the top of each cartridge, carefully poured out the lead shot and instead used roofing lead that had been cut into a strip and rolled up tightly into a solid plug. This they inserted above the gunpowder (in the top of the cartridge). 'We used to have to catch wounded, lame deer all the time and take them to the vet's to be put out of their misery,' said the sergeant. 'I've seen entry wounds the size of a tennis ball, and exit wounds like torn-open pancakes.'

One favourite way to poach pheasants used to be to follow the gamekeeper's feed line: that's the line of grain he would scatter on the ground in a clearing for the pheasants. You took a fishing line and laid it out where the pheasants were in the habit of feeding. Every two feet along the line, you tied on a side-shoot with a fishing hook on the end, baited with a raisin. Raisins are irresistible to pheasants, and once the birds had hooked themselves, the poacher returned and silently pulled in the line and the pheasants.

Most of the real action in the country takes place under cover: it's deceit or crafty dissembling of some kind. During the day-time, everyone in the village and even in the fields feels they are under surveillance. Night-time is different: it is the traditional time for poaching and skulduggery of various kinds. Darkness offers a respite from the neighbours' spotlight attention.

The new collection of essays by Eric Rolls. If my house had a belfry, I would be ringing peals of bells for this book. As it is, I fell on it when it arrived as a man does after Ramadan or a forty days' fast.

You still can't buy the collected essays of Les Murray in Britain. What is going on? How can the greatest poet of our times have his essays out of print in a civilized, English-speaking country? Why is Britain so blind to the glories of Australian writing? And, in particular, its glorious ecological writing?

The naturalness of an unnatural product. The great chrome Jaguar over the entrance to Marshall's garage showroom opposite the airfield at Cambridge. The early motor car names were all about grace and speed: Swallow, Jaguar, Alvis Silver Eagle, Singer Gazelle, Humber Super Snipe (Reliant Robin or Reliant Scimitar, you take your choice).

Or status: Austin Cambridge, Morris Oxford.

Or more aggressive: the AC Cobra, the Grinnall Scorpion, with a sting in its tail – something you had better watch out for. The Chevrolet Stingray. They were the precursor of the present rash of 4WDs, SUVs. We will pass over the Jaguar SS.

28th February

Another very cold, snowy day. I peel oranges and place the peel on top of the wood-burner in my study, and their drying out perfumes the room with orange musk.

In the afternoon I feel so much better than I have done all week that I go outside to a coppiced ash tree growing near the bank of the front moat and bend its poles into a series of spirals, held in position by wooden stakes driven into the soft ground. Ash is by far the most muscular and resilient of trees, and I love to feel its resistance as I wrestle each pole into shape, gripping it in an armlock, and flexing it almost to the limit of its pliability.

March.

1st March

Cowpasture Lane Inquiry. I tried to make the case that in the Middle Ages people were on the land – on it, in it – in a way that we simply are not today. We live our lives outside the land. We stay off it, mostly.

The strange thing about the Cowpasture Lane Public Inquiry was how very private it actually was. For most of the two days of the sitting we, the villagers, sat as mute spectators to the abstruse process: a barrister's attempt to pick holes in the case the County Council legal department had made for the status of Cowpasture Lane as a byway.

To anyone with much knowledge of the outlines of the local history of Mellis, it would have been fairly obvious that the lane was a market road leading to three neighbouring markets at the villages of Burgate, Botesdale and Redgrave.

What happened at the inquiry was that a small number of lawyers, County Council people, the lawyer for the objectors and another lawyer from Railtrack all pored over legal documents and maps at one end of the hall. The leading objector in the village, Lieutenant-Colonel Spence, even referred to the villagers present as 'the audience'. There was an outraged gasp at this, but in a way he was right. None of us was a legal expert, so we were relegated to the sidelines.

I wrote in my evidence that until about 1850 the lane would have been the main road into the village, and that, with the coming of the railway about then, the whole axis of the village moved over to the eastern end of the common. The barrister asked me if I stood by the statement. Since writing it nearly a year ago, I had realized that in fact the village axis had already begun to shift west, away from mill, church, school and well, to a part of the huge common over half a mile away. There were in effect two villages, just as there were Thornham Magna and Parva, and Burgate Great and Little Green and Mellis Little Green. There were even two different Lords of the Manor.

This may possibly have occurred because of the plague, or it may simply have been some organic movement, a sort of natural gregariousness – you could be far closer as neighbours around a relatively small green. So the lane probably became far less busy than at its heyday in the thirteenth century, when it would have been a busy market road.

I wanted to explain how important all the immediately surrounding villages and towns were. I wanted to point out that Hoxne was where St Edmund was martyred, that in 869 a great religious procession carried his remains to rest at the abbey at Beadoriceworth, thenceforth known as Bury (or Burgh) St Edmunds. On the walls of Thornham Parva Church the martyrdom of St Edmund is depicted in an early painting. It is possible that the procession, which would have taken a ceremonial route, not simply the most direct, passed from Hoxne to Eye (an abbey), and thence to Thornham Parva. We know that at the end of the first day's procession, the bier and its bearers paused to spend the night at Burgate, where a church was built. This is the origin of its name: 'gate', meaning 'the way to', as in 'Burgate' – 'the way to Bury'.

If the funeral procession had gone via Eye and Thornham Parva, then it is more than likely it would have passed down Cowpasture Lane, crossed the common and gone up Stonebridge Lane into Burgate.

The main problem about the inquiry for me was that the inspector had not walked the lane before it began. It meant that we were talking all the time about a place that was, for her, an abstraction. None of the experts round the table knew any of the rest of the village. And, most seriously of all, none of them knew the common and the system of lanes that funnel in and out of it to all the neighbouring villages, settlements and commons. They only wanted to focus on Cowpasture Lane itself; nothing else. They didn't want to take a holistic view of the common and its system of associated lanes and long greens as a single organic entity.

4th March
Snowfall and settling – three to four inches.

I have to admit to a lifelong habit of liking to form bonds with animals. Just now as I write, there's a cock pheasant outside my window devouring a slice of bread I threw out for him in the snow. It is snowing hard, and the pheasant is a dignified, blurred figure, like Shackleton, only in full morning dress. Snow settles on his russet back, so he must be warm inside his feathers. Cornflakes, confetti, paperweights, pixels, interference. I think of a favourite garden plant my mother always grew: snow-in-the-mist. A snowstorm is a mist: the further away you try to focus, the more snowflakes come between you and, say, a tree. It's only logical.

I look up the chimney and snowflakes are floating down, vivid against the soot inside – as though white were drawn to black by an attraction of opposites.

A walk in the snow up Stonebridge Lane to the Plantation Wood and Whitmore's Wood. A wood in the snow shows up well – dark trunks against the white, and there's more light in it, reflected.

There's a wood bank up there – it is a plantation – with silver birches and cherries, not local species. But across to the right, in the wood that was cut down and replanted in awful straight lines, there are lovely big furze bushes in flower in the snow, and other local old species reasserting themselves.

In the field, six white bottoms of roe-deer in a row. Michael [Battell's] farm is a single, huge white plain – not a hedge in sight. The flints of an old wood-entrance branch off the lane.

When I moved here in the 1970s, the whole of Suffolk was in disarray: barns were being pulled down, old cottages demolished with nothing more than a Land Rover or tractor and a stout length of cable. Farmers spoke matter-of-factly in the pub about the barns they demolished.

I begin pollarding the oak by the vegetable garden. I ponder the word 'nasty' as applied to oak by Forster in his first description of the wych-elm in *Howards End*. Why is the oak 'no nastier than ordinary oaks'? It saws easily, the branches cut cleanly in March, they aren't sappy yet, although the buds are just beginning to redden and swell. But the hairiness of the oak tree is notable: the profusion of little side-shoots all the way up the trunk. It is almost prickly, and this could be said to be nasty. Most of all, it tastes nasty to herbivores because it is full of tannin.

The little apple trees in the vegetable garden are just beginning to show their pink terminal buds and to open them into tiny leaves. The roses, little Kyrgyz too, are coming into leaf.

Visceral – is when your hair stands on end, when your teeth are set on edge by nails on a blackboard, when you experience a kind of sympathetic reaction, such as when a man with an artificial leg sits down opposite you across a café and gets it caught on a chair as he manoeuvres in behind his table. Such things catch at you in unexpected parts of the body – like foot massage, when a tweaked big toe can tweak you in the testicles.

9th March

I've been doing all the usual lonely-man things tonight, ringing up friends all over the world and hanging on the phone for hours. Reading alone, eating a big plate of spaghetti alone. Not drinking alone, although I thought of it.

13th March

New moon. Last night the cats had a magic about them, a new devilment in their eyes. Their fur flooded up over their body – waves went through their fur – physical waves. They went out and stood on the kitchen step, peering into the night, twisting their whiskers. All was still.

When I picked up the kettle to fill it this morning, there was the very first ant of the year, exploring the butcher's block in the kitchen, pondering crystals of sugar with its antennae.

Everything has its antennae out at full stretch, fully extended.

In the sunny outside loo, writing this with the door open, and Alfie sitting outside, the first gnat flies aimlessly about.

These are the outriders of spring.

The great spotted woodpecker – a completely medieval bird, like a joker, or a jester with mask, cap and bells. The black and white skullcap, the deep red velvet tail, the barred, flamboyant costume and the outsized conk of a beak, absurdly vigorous in its hammering. How on earth does it stabilize its brain?

What joy, after weeks of cold grey days, to get out the tractor. Today, I back it out of the shed, hear the music of its engine burst into life, hook up the old two-wheel elm-sided trailer and trundle off down the field for wood, having waded up with chainsaw, hard-hat, fuel, chain oil, bow-saws, billhooks and a selection of hedging gloves. In the wood, I coppiced two hazels with the chainsaw. The tall poles fell outwards like a star around each coppice stool and lay on the floor of the wood. I then set to work with the short-handled billhook, stripping off the side branches, trimming the feathery tops of the poles and laying them together as neatly as the pencils on my desk (in a pile). Keith [Dunthorne] had shown me how to hold the work over the fresh-cut coppice stool, so that the cut ends fall directly on to it, building up into a loose protective cage through which the new shoots will grow straight up towards the light, safe from the rubbing of deer, hares or rabbits.

I was thus engaged with my billhook when my aim went awry and the sharp, glancing blade sliced straight through the leather glove and cut a choice fillet out of the ball of my thumb. The sudden sharp pain, the surprise and shock, then instant self-recrimination, are all still vivid enough. But what really struck home was the immediate and overwhelming realization that this is what it feels like for the tree. It was a real moment of inscape, as Gerard Manley Hopkins called it, a sudden illuminating impulse of sympathy with, in this case, the hazel tree, the living, green hazel bough. Only the night before I had been reading Hopkins's poem 'Binsey Poplars'. The red sap welled up and began to trickle over the glove. I took it off gingerly and bound my handkerchief tightly round the thumb, literally grafting the severed flesh back on.

As I walked back up the field to the first-aid box in the workshop, I ran through the Hopkins poem in my head, and felt the hurt he felt, as I always do, but this time throbbing in my own fragile flesh.

> O if we but knew what we do
> When we delve or hew –
> Hack and rack the growing green!

I myself felt 'hacked and racked', and the healing of my bandaged thumb would now be linked with the healing of the coppiced hazel trees through a kind of sympathetic magic.

As I worked, I reflected that even the brushwood I was leaving behind me heaped over the coppice stools would, in former times, have been bundled into faggots, brought under cover and stacked to dry for fuel to bake bread.

Hazel too has skin. It comes out of the wood, and is misted matt-green with algae. The smooth, delicate brown bark can be polished to a high sheen when you work with hazel rods in the carpentry shop. It will peel too, though nothing like as readily as a birch, and, twisted up, it has a certain strength as twine, though nothing like as strong as the bark of lime.

It has the same freckled skin type as the birch family. The leaves of hazel are the cling film of our grandmothers, and still used to wrap cheeses in France, Italy or Greece. I used to make goat's cheese here and always wrapped my cheeses in hazel leaves to keep them moist and succulent. Hazel leaves aren't toxic, as clingfilm is said by some to be, and as packaging, what could be more beautiful?

So here I am, with a chainsaw, spending an afternoon amputating the limbs of trees. 'Tree surgery', they sometimes call it. I have chosen a mild day, when the forecast is for even milder weather. I want to avoid cutting trees when frost could damage the new wounds – the wound is living tissue and must heal.

'Consideration' is the word my parents always used. 'Have some consideration' was the phrase, or 'Show some consideration', a slightly different thing, so I was taught to raise the peak of my school cap to passing neighbours in the street, to give up my seat on the underground train to just about anyone unfortunate enough to be standing. Ladies, certainly, and older people. There's sense in this. Who needs to sit down when they're seven years old and bursting with energy?

This basic idea of consideration is at the heart of all true conservation. You act out of consideration, out of fellow feeling, for other living things, and other people. Most of the degradation of our land, air and water is caused by selfishness.

Selfishness and consideration. These are the two opposites that were constantly before me as choices when young. Should I do the selfish thing, fire my airgun through the neighbour's garden fence, perforating it almost to destruction? Or should I do the considerate thing and fire it dutifully at the target pinned to a tree? Or not fire it at all? I confess I enjoyed shooting very much and only gave it up when I had 'worked it out of my system'.

When I gashed my thumb and the blood spurted, I couldn't help feeling a hint of the pleasure I used to feel, or pride, at bleeding when I was a boy. 'Who's a wounded soldier, then?' my mother would say.

16th March
Yesterday it turned mild for the first time in ages and last night I found a newt crossing the kitchen floor at some speed. On

Sunday night I saw frogs and toads crossing the road, catching one in the headlights at Syleham by the Waveney, and another on the common at Mellis. At Thrandeston, where there's a notable frog pond on the village green, two people were fixing up a road sign with a crossed-out frog on it, and this morning the first toads are in full voice beside the moat.

The first bumblebees are out foraging. It is sunny and still, after all the wind. Birds are singing in the hedges. A single pair of sparrows nesting – in the roof probably – and visiting the peanut dispenser outside my study window.

Once, in Suffolk, the *i*'s were all undotted and the *t*'s all uncrossed. Now everyone's busy crossing all the *t*'s and dotting all the *i*'s in the landscape.

The old thatched garage at Redgrave, gently rotting and derelict for years, is now being rebuilt.

At the swimming pool, I met my friend Ken Burrell, the history teacher at the high school in Diss. He used to take a hiking party of Fifth and Sixth Formers to the Lakes every Easter, and I went with him several times. He is a superb hill-walker, always fit, and highly experienced. He knows the mountains and the lakes backwards, every inch, and we would always climb Helvellyn, Great Gable, Scafell, run the scree at Wastwater, bike up Borrowdale, etc. etc. Now, he has received a letter from the Norfolk Education Authority telling him he isn't allowed to take any pupils higher than 2,000 feet unless he has been on a special mountain course and got a certificate. So this year, for the first time in twenty-five years or so, he won't be taking anyone to the Lakes.

It is the same for other schools of course, so the lakes and mountains of Cumbria will be relatively quiet this Easter, and future generations of school students will be deprived of an important part of their education.

The human relationship with farm animals is fundamentally a deceit. It is a betrayal of the animals' trust, since all the time, as the farmer nurtures them, and their trust in him deepens, he is concealing in his heart a murderous intention.

To murder your own family like this requires a high degree of ruthlessness, or denial, or both.

I want all my friends to come up like weeds, and I want to be a weed myself, spontaneous and unstoppable. I don't want the kind of friends one has to cultivate.

Timber-framed houses leave very little remains. Any useful timbers are taken and reused, or burnt as firewood. Any bricks or tiles would certainly be gathered, or sold, and reused elsewhere. That leaves only thatch, which might be burnt, or just rot down.

This afternoon I resumed pollarding the oak at the corner of the vegetable garden. I used the big bow-saw to cut through the trunk 8' 6" above the ground, leaving three big branches intact beneath it. The green oak pinched the saw blade halfway through, and I had to hammer in a wedge behind the saw to open up the cut and free up the saw. It was very tough going. I counted the rings in the sawn-off trunk, and there were something between eighteen and twenty. The tree has yielded a lot of underwood – faggots, kindling, etc.

18th March

Bike ride – impossible to remain at my desk today, it is so warm and full of spring! Fieldfares clacking and churring in the ash-tops, driven off the common by the village school cross-country race. The fatties all bringing up the rear, and after less than half a mile many of them are walking.

The common has been invaded by a great rash of luminous yellow: hundreds of police traffic cones on our country road, and dozens of marshals in luminous waistcoats (we always used sticks to mark out the course).

In Burgate Wood, on a wide lane along one side of the wood. Ash coppice now fenced with wire netting as a pheasant area. Coppice hornbeams seem to gesture like hands thrown up generously, or the ash coppice like fingers thrust up through mud – the fingers of a drowning man. Hazel coppice like sea anemones. I snorkel through.

The polished steel, the gun barrels of hornbeam. Grey gun-metal, gleaming and polished.

A small pile of old bottles, farm horse medicine mostly, under a tree round the roots. Wood banks everywhere up to six feet deep or more. Massive in their day. Ash stools ten feet long and wide.

I am fooled by a purple chocolate wrapper into diving for an early violet.

Looking, just looking, is all we have to do, to see the essential truth. This is all Turner did, with his travelling palette.

Primroses are up, so are celandines. The verges pinned with celandines.

25th March

Toads croaking tonight in the pond at one end of the moat. A clear sky, bright moon, just a puff or two of Santa's beard cloud.

This afternoon I went into Burgate Wood with Alison [Hastie] and we found oxlips in the rides. Low pollards of hornbeam, cut at three or four feet off the ground. One huge old hornbeam pollard you could stand inside with ten great poles.

We found the mound site of the original hall, huge moats, the site now full of coppice hazel and ash. Stumps of very old oaks, all split into pages like books. Huge cratered coppice stools of hornbeam and ash. Nettles on the site of the old hall where the midden was.

At sunset, Alison thinks she sees a bonfire across the far side of the wood, but it's a burning wedge of the setting sun, seen between two trees. It is due west down a ride, exactly opposite the full moon, already risen next to Burgate Church.

Lichens in ashes, including a weird cancerous one that sends the branches mad and 'hairy'. Deer damage to young ashes and the bark of hornbeam.

A patch of wild redcurrant bushes. A memorial stone to Jimmy Hammond, 'who worked on the estate for 50 years' – died 1998 – at 'Jimmy's Ride'.

Hazels that have got away into trees with trunks six or eight inches in diameter like birches.

Some singled oaks with big swollen bases where they were once coppiced.

Too many deer, not enough woods.

At Burgate, the ash that grows entirely round the iron fence is eighteenth- or nineteenth-century – and grafts its own branches together.

The baling twine of the old gamekeeper's gibbet is still there. Dead stoat on the ground – or was it a squirrel?

Much as I enjoy the process of writing and the exercise of my own skill and craft in getting it right, none the less I would often prefer to be a jotter.

Jottings, in their spontaneity and complete absence of any craft, are often so much truer to what I actually feel or think at a given moment.

29th March
Brilliant swimming day – essentially chilly, but very warm in the sun, gardening like mad, lighting a bonfire – a good one of blackthorn, and prunings from various plums behind the barn and outside lavatory, and roses and bushes and vines round the garden walls. The bike ride into a cool north-easterly light breeze slowed me down, and it took forty minutes, not thirty. The wood people have moved in properly and cut down some of the trees to make more space and laid a double rampart of plaited hedge.

What a dastardly tool is the strimmer – hardly a glimmer.

30th March

A huge, sweeping, grass-trembling wind, swaying every tree and playing fugues along the hedgerows. It clatters the tops of the willows together like hockey sticks and beats down all the dead twigs. It carries down dead boughs from the ash and tears off sallow boughs.

The cries of boys float in from the wide ocean of the common, where they ride their skateboards before the wind, making sails of their anoraks by spreading their arms like yardarms.

The wind has demolished my polytunnel, tearing the polythene at the brittle seams and ripping it off. Blue tits cling to the peanut feeders hanging wildly from a garden plum tree, feeding nonchalantly as they're thrown about violently, riding the storm. The bamboo is laid nearly flat, showing the silver sides of its leaves like white flags of surrender.

Then, as darkness falls, so does the rain, lashings of it. Then hail, battering, clattering, on the northward windows out of the black night.

All night the wind toils round the house and in the trees and hedges, tugging the ash tree this way and that, dancing its branches like a puppet, shaking and tugging at it as children do with puppets.

Suffolk used to be much more public, communal in feel and life. It used to be hillbilly country. Now it is private.

April.

2nd April

The source of a river, a tear duct of the earth.

The source of a river is always a matter of particular fascination. Its very mention brings out the explorer in all of us.

I have wandered into a small, rushy field in Redgrave, where sheep graze and the paraphernalia of shepherding is strewn about the field. There's an ooze in the ground, a wet patch that squelches as you walk over it.

A sparse thinning of birches and sallows. It is a source of the Little Ouse, and the Waveney. Redgrave Fen.

The brook at Heveningham that runs down from outside the Low House at Laxfield becomes the Blyth, and the great Blyth Estuary at Blythburgh.

In Gittings Wood. Strong, cold, north wind blowing. I go up the side of the field, uphill, and cross over a young wheat field to the wood. It has a wood bank and a deep ditch, and as soon as I enter the wood I am struck by the enormous carpet of lily-of-the-valley leaves, and wood anemone in flower, studded with the deep blue of violets. Bluebell leaves, and, further into the wood, herb Paris. Also town hall clock, and blotched leaves of the early purple orchid – hundreds of them, many browsed by deer, flowers just beginning to bud. Primroses, although not very plentiful. Very big ash stools, a few hornbeam stools at the south-west end of the wood. Mostly very high ash coppice that has shot up forty or fifty feet and sways about in the wind, the tops crashing and clattering, and the sound of the wind about and outside the wood.

Clacking of the ash stems together. Many ash stools six or eight feet wide, and several open circular stools.

8th April

I am well on the way to becoming a tree myself. I put down roots. I sigh when the wind blows. My sap rises in the spring, and I turn towards the sun. My skin even begins to look more like bark every day. Which tree would I be? Definitely a walnut; an English walnut, *Juglans regia*, the tree with the greatest canopy.

Conservation can only concern itself with what is past and gone, not with the future. Yet, if that is the case, why flood new wetlands in the hope of attracting more bitterns to nest?

Why landscape Redgrave Fen in the hope of more raft spiders and otters and dragonflies? Why not devote a lot more care and attention to the wild western end of Mellis Common? It is a huge area of some seventy to eighty acres that is almost entirely free of the pressures on wildlife associated with human presence around the perimeter.

At the eastern end of the common, you have increasing numbers of people and their pet dogs and cats, all disturbing the common in one way or another.

The hedges along the common from Hall Farm to Stonebridge Lane are almost exclusively blackthorn, with elm now suckering back, some hawthorn, the odd field maple, and bramble and dog rose.

The hedges along the boundary from Stonebridge Lane west to Furzeway are, again, almost all blackthorn, with some individual hawthorn bushes or trees, a few ash, elm as the second species now suckering back and doing quite well, a single holly, two hazels at the far west end near a large ash tree, sallow, some little elder and bramble. The hedge bushes and trees have been coppiced to the ground, and a species mixture has been replanted in a different, regular pattern, to create a hedge that will eventually mature into a very different-looking 'standard conservation hedge', that is to say a mix of dogwood, hawthorn, blackthorn, field maple, holly and hazel. All these species are represented to a greater or lesser extent in other parts of the parish, but here the character of the hedge is that it is predominantly blackthorn.

Incidentally, there always was a lilac tree in this hedge, and it has now been removed. This is unpardonable. The lilac was much loved, an entirely accidental arrival (there is another in one of the hedges along Pye Meadow on the boundary of my land), and it was part of the local distinctiveness of the hedge.

William Morris's principle of repair, rather than restoration, applies to hedges. You should repair the hedge by planting what was there before; not new species or varieties.

It is a sad fact that all our recent wars have been ignominious affairs, and modern agriculture has been much the same: doing dreadful things to the land that you know in your bones are wrong, but that you end up doing, as a duty, all the same: dropping the cluster bombs, or polluting the fields and the rivers with poisons.

What we need is the farming equivalent of conscientious objectors: people who are prepared to stand up and say, 'No, we won't do this any more', at whatever personal risk.

Certain things, objects, implements, I make over and over again. Chairs for bums, spoons for lips. The love-spoons the Welsh carve so intricately out of hedge hawthorn are presented for the pleasure of the lips. I have exchanged spoons many times with a loved and adored woman, often from a far-distant country, and it is like kissing. And the chairs, so lovingly scooped and scalloped with a bespoke shave, stroking the tough grain of the elm to accommodate the desired buttocks of a loved woman.

Burgate Wood. The moated island site of the old manor is sixty yards square and raised a good six to ten feet above the level of the rest of the wood. More nettles grow on it than in the wood around it, perhaps because the ground has been disturbed, and perhaps because it is enriched with the compost and detritus of five centuries of human habitation. At one corner I stand inside a huge circular ash coppice, cratered and ruined, with a maple coppice to one side of it, both shooting up fifty feet, the crater twelve feet wide. The wood floor here is mossy and soft. Searching for just the right camping spot, I circle round and round, feeling the ground for a perfectly level place underneath the grasses, dog's mercury, nettles, blue ground ivy and, appropriately, lords and ladies.

Stepping off the island, I find myself in a dark part of the wood full of the biggest, most ancient hornbeams, all pollarded very close to the ground, no more than three or four feet up, yet with trunks twelve feet in girth.

One enormous tree, which must rise to sixty feet, throws such dense shade that beneath it is a circle of bare brown leaf mould twenty yards in circumference. The tree has thrown up twenty-one winding pollard poles, steely and serpentine, all held firm by the pitched guy-ropes of the tree roots, stretched taut on the twelve-foot-diameter trunk.

Inside, a pigeon nest, the bare skull of a rabbit, picked clean, perhaps, by a hawk. It must have carried the rabbit head to the nest and devoured it safely off the ground.

The ghost of the manor house on its raised bosky mound haunts me. For five centuries, the De Burgate family inhabited this place. The nettles are signs of their occupation, their night soil, discarded bones and seashells, their compost and even their old clothes. The rags of time. I found an ancient whelk shell, tossed from a banqueting table eight hundred years ago, dissolved to a fragile chalky filament in the bank of the moat.

Deciding on a place to sleep, I went round and round in circles like a cat about to curl up in the sunshine. This circling into a nest must be something all mammals share, a subtle appraising of the terrain, assessing the minor but crucial questions of the presence of a molehill, an outcrop of flint or a clump of nettles. I wanted a dry spot as high as possible above the surrounding wood, and chose a natural dish of earth in the shade of a ruined and cratered coppice stool, an atoll of verdant leaf mould, surrounded by a reef of apparently rotten wooden islets that somehow sprouted huge muscular poles of ash that wove their way diagonally upwards towards gaps in the canopy.

Little things assume a greater importance at such times: the knuckle of root that could press into your ribs and keep you awake all night; the angle of your view into the rest of the wood, and on to the moat, a watering hole.

Lidos are more fun than swimming pools. Lidos are to swimming pools what cathedrals are to churches. They are much more fun, they leave a lasting impression, and they cost a lot more to do up these days. 'Fun' is the word you immediately associate with lidos. Nobody here can ever quite agree whether to say 'Leedo' or 'Liedo' (a place for lying down in the sun). It is one of those words, like 'toilet' that we have borrowed from the Continentals, and tried unsuccessfully to Anglicize. 'Toilet' sounds much better as *toilette* in the original French. And 'lido' sounds much better in the original Italian.

I remember how upset the commoners of Dungeness – Dunge Beach – were at someone moving in and fencing off a piece of the beach next door to Derek Jarman's cottage. Jarman made his garden – but a wild one in a wild way, which would shade off into the wilderness of the beach, into the natural profusion of plants growing there.

Little picket fences have begun to appear all over the local commons – Wortham Ling, Wortham Long Green – fencing off bits of 'take' – poached land.

13th April
A voyage by bike down Stubbings Lane in Burgate/Ricking-hall. A really wild, *Rogue Male*-ish lane full of dense thickets of blackthorn. A blackthorn jungle, a stockade, armoured by

lethal venomous thorn as painful and threatening as anything Australia can offer.

I turned off the little side road by a modern steel-clad barn standing on its own at the top of a low hill near Burgate Wood and Burgate Little Green. I cycled down the uneven track of a green lane, fringed by hedges and trees, mostly blackthorn and elm, now suckering back again into new life. Field maple, dog rose, dogwood. The lane ran downhill and turned to the left, where it opened out into a 'long green', a wide area of grazing, now partly colonized by blackthorn, which enclosed little grassy glades where odd discarded car wheels and batteries suggested travellers had camped here in the recent past. A small blackthorn forest. Sound of chiffchaff song. Perhaps blackcaps later on. The lane continued for a long way: through Stubbings Green, with the sites of more than one extinct house or barn (Imple House and Procter's Barn no longer exist, yet are shown on the 1926 Ordnance Survey). The apparently lifeless floor of a blackthorn copse – impenetrable, the avalanche of blossom on top. A sloe paradise in winter, November/December.

Puddles, a stream becoming almost a rivulet with the strong brown flow of recent rains, brooklime, stitchwort, fool's watercress along its banks, cowslips and primroses by the track. Then a huge long-felled oak tree lying on its side in the hedge. Why did no one plank it up into timber? Its presence is a sign of the relative affluence of the Suffolk farmers: they couldn't really be arsed to haul the tree out to the sawmill.

I eventually emerged from the lane to discover a brick-built warehouse building that might have been a power station but obviously wasn't, and a pair of farms, badlands places with all the signs of bad farming and outlaw backwoods enterprise – broken farm machinery in a great dump on a concrete pad, more concrete, an old derelict Land Rover, its blue paint washed out by acid rain to a streaked pale blue, and a series of huge open-sided sheds filled with mountains of black spent mushroom compost. A whole mountain range of it in heaps outside on yet more concrete pads and an ancient Hymac digger that once belonged to 'J. Green & Son, Yarmouth'. The inhabitants of the farm had obviously had dealings with garden centres, because representatives of all the least likely trees and bushes to plant round a Suffolk farmhouse in the depths of the wild had been planted everywhere: eucalyptus, pampas grass, and a 25-foot-high date palm grew at one end of the house. How it had survived the Suffolk winters I don't know.

A sudden warm, sunny day after a long, very cold, frosty spell. Full moon shining on the new blossoming plum in the garden, moon reflected in the perfectly still moat on a clear, perfectly still night. An American bomber plane flies straight towards the garden high overhead, its three lights shining forward, so the plum seems illuminated from both sides: by the moon to its right, and by the US Air Force, returning from Iraq, to its left.

Distant barn owl in Thornham Wood, and the toads in the moat, like old men snoring in an upstairs room as I walk home from the pub down a village street. Distant toads, distant owls.

The magic of outdoor skating is all too rare a pleasure these days. As a child, I remember skating all the time every winter. As soon as winter clamps down with a big frost, you are in another world.

One great source of the magic must be that you are walking on water. Then, as you acquire some skill in the art, the joys of flight. The sheer pleasure of flying across the ice. Some of the record times in the fenland skating races have been extraordinary – 2½-minute mile in 1885.

The experience of skating is so intense that it stays with you. The cold frosty wind rushes into your face, up your nostrils. The whole pond becomes a musical instrument, with the ice as its sounding board. There is a music of skates, a rhythmic 'swish' as the blades cut through the virgin surface of the black ice.

Looking down into the ice, studying it, the little bubbles fossilized, trapped in mid eruption. The sheer contrast of the static, frozen world of ice with the explosions of energy and movement in the skaters.

There is always a special magic because it is available only as a rare, occasional pleasure. Hence, it is romantic: an extreme case of that very English thing – deferred gratification. For that reason, it is all the more memorable.

Weather conditions, too, are extreme – and the body responds to the cold with vigorous secretions of hormones and endorphins.

The world is made vivid by the reflected light of snow and ice. Skating is one of those words that may be relied upon to trigger a flood of memories.

On Mellis Common, which has twenty-four ponds, there was always skating – and at night, after the farm work was done, the villagers would gather with lanterns and Billy Battell's old wind-up gramophone and skate and skate. Also at Dickleburgh, on the water meadows – shallow and flooded. Big bonfire on one side to illuminate the ice.

Memories – somehow it is the vividness and freedom that we remember more than the chilblained toes, or bruised knees or sacral vertebrae. I long ago acquired the knack of padding up well with several layers of trousers before venturing on to the ice. Not only wrapping up but padding up too.

Skates echoing across the ice in early-morning frost before the ice is powdered by the passage of too many skates.

The shouts of joy or alarm, scarves, gloves, the elaborate lacing of boots.

Clearing out my workshop the other day I came across a pair of my old ice skates. From time to time at our local auction room a pair of skates comes up for sale, cobwebbed and little used these days.

One of the pleasures of English weather is that the big freeze, like the heatwave, is always a possibility and speaks of holiday.

It is the child, the subversive part, in all of us who longs for the moment when the weather brings everything to a standstill and we can go out tobogganing, sliding, snowballing or skating.

The way birds fly. We should use onomatopoeia much more to describe their flight. A rook flying flippy-floppy, dippy-doppy wings splashing around in the sky like a dog-paddler.

I don't have a problem with anger, I have a problem with the things that make me angry, and I think the main problem I have is that most people – society in general – are not sufficiently angry about those things that upset me. That in itself makes me angry – a sort of latter-day angry young man.

14th April
Sunny, warmer, bee-flies on the aubrietia. A hedgehog poo near the kitchen door. Maybe he's woken up already? The oily courtship song of the greenfinch, like the swinging open of a well-oiled door. Ducks sleeping on the lawn, heads tucked in.

15th April
A Drones' Club of mallard drakes on the lawn, all lying about and preening.

I would choose starlings to work for me if I had a bird-building job to do. They are so muscular and determined – and greedy for life too.

Jackdaws come to this spinney along the edge of the common and take twigs for their nests. I've watched them for years in spring, flying to and fro from their nests in the tower of Burgate Church, a mile away, to the spinney on the common, a goldmine of dead twigs.

'A host of golden dandelions.' I wipe a puddle of rainwater off the oilskin on my garden table and decide to count the dandelion heads. Just how many daffodils were there in that host of them that Wordsworth describes? It may sound obsessive, but I want to get better at judging, rather than guessing, the number of dandelions on a field, or gulls in a passing flock, or swallows wheeling over my garden.

19th April

I watch a hoverfly alight on a clematis flower and explore its stamens for pollen. It reminds me of *Microcosmos* and I think, yes, it really is another world, this microscopic insect world, a world apart. But almost at once I realize that to put insects into 'another world' or 'a world apart' is dangerous. In fact it is the rationale for exterminating them with pesticides. If theirs is 'another world', it has nothing to do with us. It is unconnected, and, whatever we choose to do to it, we ourselves are unaffected. The very reverse is the truth, of course. Unless we realize we share a single world with the insects, and that if we harm them we harm ourselves and the rest of nature, we will end up destroying ourselves – committing suicide, in fact.

Grandpa Wood was brought up by foster-parents Rebecca George and Mr George. He was born in Chase Terrace or Chase Town – or at least grew up there. His father was Wood of Brockhurst-Wood, a timber firm in Walsall. Later, the family lived at No. 5, The Avenue, Truro. The Fentons had a big store in Walsall – a general store that grew into a department store.

Grandpa Wood worked at the Cannock & Rugeley Colliery as time-keeper and wages clerk – after the accident in which he lost his right hand.

20th April

Good Friday. Chaffinches chirping their regular squeaky-machine song, the sunny, warm air filled with the hum of bumblebees and wood pigeons. They have paired up and are swooping high, cooing in their special 'whoopee-we-are-flying-for-fun' song. Wood pigeons wind the handle of their cyclical song, halfway or three quarters, then just leave go and let their song hang inconclusively in the air.

The moat has warmed up to 15°C – so just warm

enough for a reasonable dip. Water quality improving with the sunshine and light. I dipped in the net, and there are plenty of giant water snails, and several newts, and the first water-boatmen and pond skaters. Garden bluebells are out, so are cowslips, a solitary hyacinth, the aconites, dog's mercury.

I walked down Cowpasture Lane and marvelled at the variety of blackthorn and wild plum and bullaces, and the difference in their blossoms. There is no more magnificent sight in Cowpasture Lane than a mountain of snowy blackthorn blossom in the sun against a pure blue sky, and a peacock butterfly enjoying the flowers.

Saw a speckled wood butterfly on dog's mercury too. The trouble with 'scrub clearance' is that the dog's mercury goes mad and takes over from gentler shade-lovers like primrose, stitchwort, violet (especially), and then the cow-parsley takes over, especially where the horses were allowed far too long to graze, and then the blackberry – brambles rush in where the blackthorn used to be and smother it.

A pair of jays were in the lane, making a strange sound I thought must be foxes, or growling cats. Magpies silently snooping for birds' nests, a crow, and a warbler, I think, was the blackcap in the big greengage tree by the outside loo this morning. Each time I set up to record them they went away or went silent as soon as I began.

They say when you lay a hedge the branches should always be sloping upward, yet ash trees disobey the rule by growing their lateral branches out, then swooping down, then up again at the tips like chandeliers.

The ash beside the old pollard oak by the curved pond is fifteen feet taller, yet hasn't lost any branches at all. The oak, which must be less supple, has had several big limbs torn off by the winter winds.

21st April

I am on a morning bike ride in sunny and suddenly warmer weather because the wind has gone round into the south or south-west.

Riding down Green Lane near Gislingham. Stitchwort – white dots punctuating the picture – cowslips and the bloody hoof-craters left by the horse-riders who are turning our parish landscape into a leisure park – throwing me off my bike. And crab-apple blossom bursting from a hedge where it has been cut and pruned back into the hedge as though it were a bush. An explosion of blossom.

The frayed ends of the hedge on the common caused by the 'bush-whacker'. Too painful to look. People say 'it's a bodged job' but actually the bodgers were doing a good job by comparison with these hedge-flaying machines and the all-important ATTITUDE they exemplify: 'Don't care, shan't care.'

As I cycle closer to Burgate Wood, I notice an increase in the number of cowslips, stitchwort, honeysuckle, primroses in the hedgerows. Ambassadors from the wood, they have spread out.

On a bike ride, you can stop and talk to people. Compliment a man on his vegetable garden or allotment plot, learn more, strike up conversation.

I can always tell the direction of the wind from my bike ride.

The outriders of a hedge still persist even when it's been razed – wild hops, bryony, elms spring stubbornly from the roots, maple, dead-nettles, stitchwort, primroses.

Suddenly the bluebells are out in the old rectory garden, and as I cycle past the rookery there's a great pool of tyre-flattened bird shit, a white pool of road-marking.

Dead-nettles, the delight of spring bumblebees – and pylons, still here blotting the landscape after nearly a hundred years. E. M. Forster objected to them. How ugly they must have looked then; they're bad enough now.

A wildlife painting should have the ring of truth – like T. H. White's hare 'with ears like funnels of ventilation shafts of a steamer'. Originality. A way of seeing, the making of connections – Mary Newcomb. A way of articulating an unconscious thought, something hitherto unspoken until now. Lichens dappling an oak trunk.

See poems of Ted Hughes and D. H. Lawrence. Clare wrote, 'I found the poems in the fields / And only wrote them down.' That's exactly what a wildlife painter does at their best. The artist doesn't just sit in the studio waiting for the painting to come to him – and nor do I when I write this piece – I shake it out of myself on a bike ride.

If only all the new houses in our village were being built of timber and cob, locally grown in working woods, and the cob dug to form new ponds, which would soon fill with water and life. Think of the dragonflies and newts, the frogs and toads. And think of the beauty of the houses, and how naturally they would fit into the village landscape. The materials are the important thing. There is no reason at all why the designs of these houses should not be far more modern and innovative and original. The problem is that the planners have focused their attention on design, instead of on materials, and have missed the point about the truly vernacular.

23rd April

First cuckoo at Mellis. Bike ride 7.55–8.25 a.m. It was a brilliant clear morning and, as I looked up at the full hawthorn all covered in ivy that grows on the common just outside the house, I thought of a date palm and of how we often project the identities of exotic plants or animals on to our own native species as a way of expressing their newness and magic. Thus Waterton and his magpies as 'English birds of paradise'. I looked across the common to the morning sun whitening the branches of the poplar opposite and thought it could be eucalyptus – a ghost gum.

Today, I've had a big panic, been thrown into deep confusion by my inability to find my two Rotring Art Pens.

I remember taking them out of the pocket of my rucksack because it had a hole in it, but I don't know where I put them. Can't see them anywhere. I cleared my desks in the study, searched all pockets of my jackets and coats, even trousers. Not a sign. I looked in the car, etc. I get very anxious when I can't find things, especially pens, the tools of my trade. Yet here I am writing with a perfectly good pen. Perfectly good, except that it isn't my Rotring Art Pen. But why do I always need to have more than one of things? It must be my deep fear of loss. My assumption that I am going to lose things or people leads to a need to protect myself, insure myself, against the loss of one pen by owning two or three. It's the same with shoes, or my computer. I'm scared of losing things and of the pain of loss. It is unbearable to me, so I hedge my bets against it, and double up.

I need someone to fold the sheet; someone to take the other end of the sheet and walk towards me and fold once, then step back, fold and walk towards me again. We all need someone to fold the sheet. Someone to hitch on the coat at the neck. Someone to put on the kettle. Someone to dry up while I wash.

Woodcraft gives wood a new life. The willow wands harvested from the Somerset Levels by the willow-men in Kingsbury Episcopi are turned into rods and woven into baskets, or, ironically, into coffins. But in either case they have a new existence, a metamorphosis into a new life.

A song thrush sings brightly, courageously, from the madly waving top of an ash tree as the wind blows savagely, trying all it can to unseat the bird whose song continues uninterrupted and as smooth as poured silver in its molten state. So, musically, you have the drone of the wind, and the lovely piping of the bird. The contrast is the same as that of uilleann pipes.

A treecreeper on the mulberry, arcing up its branches upside-down, testament to the feast of tiny insects living amongst the lichens on it. A jay comes to the plum tree and eyes the peanut-horde but resists temptation and flies a little way off to observe. A spotted woodpecker feeds for ten minutes on peanuts. It must have a nest somewhere and a mate to feed.

But do we disable ourselves with these machines? These computers? What better 'technology' than longhand? What more streamlined and portable than a pen, or pencil? Or a crayon or a paintbrush?

No one has ever done better than J. M. W. Turner did with a small travelling palette and a brush or two – and some water.

Look how we celebrate Andy Goldsworthy for all his deliberate simplicity – his use of piss or puddle water to make ice and weld a sculpture together.

A tree lives on air, like Hamlet: 'I eat the air, promise-crammed.'

When I planted the willow at one end of the moat, it was a sapling three feet tall, hardly thicker than my finger. I planted it when I first came here. There is a spring in the moat eleven feet below the surface, and it never lets the moat dry up or even lose its level much beyond a slight rising and falling of the tide with the seasons. The tree grew so tall that when the big winds came in the autumn it was in danger of being blown over into the water. And in summer it was so tall that, in the afternoon sun, it cast a giant shadow across the full length of the moat.

Now I understood why riverside willows are usually

pollarded. I decided to pollard it, and asked Dave and Barney, two young woodcutters, to come over and do the work. They were a marvel to watch, climbing straight up the tree and cutting off the topmost branches first, then working downwards, shortening it bit by bit.

At last it was pollarded, and I climbed the ladder and looked down on the sawn trunk and saw my life here ingrained in the tree. Each year I've lived in this place is a ring in the pale, straw-coloured trunk.

Now, two years later, it is sending up vigorous pollard branches, and looking better than ever.

24th April

Cold again and almost sunny. I am sitting listening for things beside the open door of my workroom. Millie sits out on the brick terrace, and her ears are alert and moving about all the time, detecting and following sounds.

The quince is now in full leaf and its blossom has almost finished. Yet there's not a sign of leaf or blossom on the mulberry. The ashes are flowering but not yet budding for leaf. The plums and blackthorn have all been in magnificent flower, snow-capped, all week. Blossom now subsiding. Cuckoo still singing on and off. Lady's smock is out on the common and on my lawn.

25th April

A wren tut-tutting in a bush. A blackcap and its pirouetting song. Last night a rave all night in Thornham Wood. The monotony of drum and bass, trance music.

It must have scared away the badgers in their tumulus. Tumult on a tumulus.

A warm sunny morning. Ants processing up and down the trunks of several ash trees. Every now and then two encounter each other going opposite ways: what is it they exchange? Do they feed each other? Or touch antennae in a conversation? What is being said? What booty are they seeking higher up the tree? One seemed to be carrying a dead aphid in its jaws. Are the aphids feeding off the sugars in the newly opening buds and being milked by the ants?

Each ant is a handsome, shiny machine, a perfect animal. They're walking up and down a willow stump, newly coppiced too. Is it sap or sugars, or aphids, they are after?

Toads hauling themselves up on to floating twigs in the pond on the common.

Cowslips in unprecedented numbers in the railway field and Cowpasture Meadow, colonizing where rabbits have grazed the ground bare.

Every little hawthorn leaf, framed in the doorway of the shepherd's hut, shimmers and quivers in the sunlight and breeze (light afternoon breeze). Song of the chiffchaff, wood pigeon (organ pipes muted), cascade song of the chaffinch. Chiffchaff like someone using a machine, a sewing machine perhaps.

I hear the claws of a blue tit, amplified by the soundbox of the shepherd's hut. A sound pinhole camera.

Silhouette of a butterfly outside my bedroom curtains, a shadow play.

The cutting back of the spinney would not have been so serious had parts of it not been bulldozed and had the coppice stools not been buried under a foot and a half of mud, which smothered all the wild flowers, hibernating bumblebees, etc., especially an extensive bed of violets that grew, with the more vigorous and assertive dog's mercury and lords and ladies, under the shade of the trees. There were also large numbers of celandines, now mostly smothered too.

The spinney afforded a superb roosting and nesting place for a variety of birds. Whitethroats nested in the brambles and blackthorn, and blackcaps and other warblers sang in there. It was a favourite roost for the wood pigeons and pheasants, and I miss the pheasants' clumsy fussing as they settled in at night, or called out at midnight under the frosty full moon.

The spinney has always formed part of a natural fringe of old woodland along the south flank of the common. Dog's mercury, shown to advance only eight inches a year by both Hoskins and Rackham, is well established as an indication of old woodland there.

The predominant tree species are ash, maple, hawthorn and blackthorn. There are elm saplings and goat willow, mainly around the ponds amongst the blackthorn and bramble, and occasional oak.

Bramble bushes have always been a characteristic feature here, and it has long been a tradition amongst us in Mellis to gather blackberries.

The seclusion and shelter offered by the fringe of woodland spinney is a vital feature of this part of the common. It encourages and emboldens the shy kingfishers to come and hawk about the pond before my house for newts, water beetles and small fish. I habitually observe these beautiful birds for hours, and the trees surrounding the ponds provide vital overhanging perches for the fishing birds.

Anyone who lives on the fringes of Mellis Common, especially to its south side at the western arm, will tell you what an elemental, windy place it is. The trees and bushes have always served an important function as a windbreak against the predominant west winds that roar across the wide, bare common in autumn and winter, right into April, seven months of the year. These west winds have brought down a good many trees along the south side, which continue to thrive as horizontal trees, often providing richer habitats, and better cover, than standing trees.

This was the case in the spinney that has been destroyed. What is condescendingly described as 'scrub' is to me and my neighbours a wilderness, full of mystery and magic, a place full of secret corners and dens.

When the spinney was lost, so were all the children's dens and campfire places, the moorhen nests in dead trees in the moat, the duck-nest corners under blackberries, and the cool glades where the deer lay up all day, after straying into our garden and staring musing before my workroom window. Now there is no cover at all for the deer, ducks or moorhens in this part of the common.

The Hymac digger even managed to remove the very tree, an ancient, near-horizontal hawthorn, in which the children had built their tree house. It was with some sadness that my son and I removed what remained of the tree-house boards, and the ropes they'd used as swings.

The local distinctiveness of this place is what is now at issue. I have lived beside this spinney, and delighted in it, for more than thirty years. I know from talking to many of the older residents of our village, from pre-war aerial photographs and from maps, as well as from the straightforward botanical evidence of the trees themselves and the wild flowers, that the spinney had existed undisturbed for well over fifty years, and probably for centuries before that. The many violets, the cuckoo pint, the primroses and the dog's mercury are all sure indications of a long-standing woodland tenure.

The spinney itself contains old holly trees of considerable interest, since they are of the rare variety that has no spines on its leaves. It was also full of ivy, the source of our Christmas decorations for years. Now there is none. The ivy was also an important food source for the birds, especially the wood pigeons, that thrive round here and make our spring and summer days such a delight with their gentle song.

It was a tremendous shock and sadness to discover that all the trees and wood had been burnt on two bonfires; one of these was on the common, right on top of an ancient ring of field blewits, the beautiful mauve-tinted, fawn-backed fungi that come up after the first frosts of autumn, and often in January and February too, always in cold, damp weather. Thirty years ago there were plenty of them on the common; now, except for on my own fields, they have all but disappeared, and this was the last of the faery rings.

I met Ronnie at Wormingford Church, where I mooched about in the churchyard waiting for the service to end, and noticed the varied menu of trees there, planted by a Victorian vicar – a big cedar near the redbrick tower, an apple and a kind of prunus with copper leaves opposite the entrance. Ronnie showed me the graves of John Constable's uncles in the yard. Fine view over the Stour Valley from next door to the church.

Back at the house, Bottengoms, there's a fine bank of bluebells and the deep pink of red campions on the most shaded banks of the hollow-way on the way down. I admired the garden – the forest of Japanese knotweed John Nash introduced along with the tall horsetails, the mauve irises whose name neither of us knows, the two pale peach paeony flowers, John Nash's favourite, the Gloire de Dijon rose by the door, the pink spears of bistort, pots full of geranium cuttings. Inside, a vase of cow-parsley and one of the mauve irises, and one of Ronnie's two cats, the white one, not the tortoiseshell, asleep on the kitchen sideboard on a dishcloth.

Ronnie showed me his newly painted white study, but he is still working downstairs with his old portable typewriter on John Nash's old paints table. Upstairs, a pair of exquisite chairs with plaited cane up the backs.

We pack the picnic things – my veg pie, Ronnie's tongue sandwiches, wine, etc. – and set off past the wind chimes by the door.

On the way to Tiger Hill we pass a field full of flints, astonishing numbers, beside the river, where Ronnie and Richard have found Saxon flints, arrowheads, etc. And the great house with a bricked moat round it.

Ronnie tells me about euphorbia, and how it took its name from the doctor of Alexander the Great's father – Dr Euphorbia. Later, in the bluebell woods, I learn how *Hyacinthoides non-scripta* got its name. Many other hyacinths have markings inside the flower bell that signify the Greek death-cry *Ai, ai,* as in Greek tragedy when someone dies – or when a mortal is transformed into a tree or plant and cries out *Ai, ai.* The bluebell doesn't have such markings – hence, *non-scripta.*

Back at Mellis I am splitting willow. Driving in the axe (maul) with pure Zen belief that I'll split it in one blow, *Zen and the Art of Archery* stuff, Kung Fu. The cats are growling their way up to a fight in the woodpile, where Millie has got herself caught. She has retreated to its cavernous shadowy depths as Alphonse advances on her, black tail twitching. Both cats growl, but mostly Millie. Alf doesn't care much and is twice her weight anyway. He always wins if he feels like it.

As I wheel a barrow of split logs to jigsaw into the pile up the south wall of the woodshed, there's a sudden explosion of cats, spitting and yowling and clattering in the logs.

It is cold, and ducks fly low and fast in pairs at dusk.

In the New Forest at camp, we used to run downhill with our canvas campbeds held high above our heads and jump in an attempt at human flight. This was a new, lightweight design of campbed, light enough when assembled to raise above your head and use as a wing.

28th April

Mellis Common. I photographed cowslips on the far side of the common along the bank between Hall Farm and School House. They are all notably tiny specimens – very weakly this year. Why? Numerous and dense in patches close to the edge of the bank.

Also photos of cuckoo flowers. Counted only thirty-seven specimens in the section between Cowpasture Farm and Walnut Tree Farm, with most of these at the end near CPF and very few indeed near WTF. To the west of the WTF track, there were more than twelve specimens where twenty years ago, or even ten, there were hundreds, turning the common mauve-white. Why?

When you look at the water, you look at the surface, as most of us do, most of the time. But there are literally millions of tiny creatures existing beneath the surface. So the interesting thing to do is to look beneath the surface, to inhabit that strange land. Going down into the water is just the same impulse as going up into the mountains, leaving the median territory of ordinary day-to-day life.

You could spend a lifetime studying a hedgerow, or a pond. Some years have elapsed since *Small is Beautiful*.

I've realized today, as I watch a plump female house spider securing and dragging home a fat bluebottle, that the spider is our household octopus. It has eight legs, bites its prey with poison fangs and holds it still as it pumps in paralysing poison.

30th April
Yesterday, the wind changed. It went round from north-east to south-west, and at last four swallows appeared over the house. I heard them first, then saw them flying and twittering round and round above the garden. It was like waving a magic wand: everything changed. The quince blossomed its pale pink peony flowers, the apple tree came into flower, and the cuckoo flowers on the lawn and out on the wide windswept sea of the common were in full pale mauve flower.

I have been eating the young dandelions, the fresh, sharp, tasty, new sorrel leaves, land cress and white campion leaves, which John Evelyn recommends in his herbal. Those swallows and their magic wand brought all the waving sea of cow-parsley outside my north window effervescing into a white froth of flower. The ash tree filled with goldfinches pecking at its flowers – fascinated by them – and greenfinches flitted along the hedges like English parrots.

May

5th May

A glorious, warm, sunny day. The wind in the ash and quince makes beautiful music – I record it. Just as I have everything set up and recording, the next-door dogs start barking. Bumble-bees everywhere this year, and some very interesting-looking carder bees and solitary wasps and ichneumon flies. Curious layer of larvae lying in the moat – or are they young newt tadpoles at a very early stage?

I see a frog near the moat. Orange-tip butterflies in garden on cow-parsley. Red admiral on nettles by ash sculpture. Ash-art is just beginning to leaf.

6th May

3 p.m. Met Richard walking on Wortham Common. Large meadow saxifrage out there. Everywhere soaked. Everyone on Wortham busy making their own water features out of the moat, digging it deeper with steep bare sides, linking little artificial dew ponds in front of their residences. Planting bamboos and other exotic bushes – cotoneasters, ceanothus – on the common, and mowing, mowing, mowing; or putting out their horses to graze it so tightly and mercilessly that nothing much would fail to feel disheartened. And the classic way of land-grabbing without actually appearing to do so: cantilevered decking – an unmistakably Australian effect.

All over the common, people have planted trees, and almost every one of them is an exotic: copper beech, horse chestnut, holm oak, cherry. Not one, except possibly ash, is native to the common itself. No hawthorn or blackthorn, even the oaks are out of place; early-budding specimens from Italy or Romania via the big forcing nurseries in Holland.

Evening, 9 p.m. An eclipse of the moon. It turned brick-red, drenched with the blood of Apollo, low down, full moon, south-south-east over the black hedges of Cowpasture Meadow. A clear purple-magenta sky and just a single white breadloaf cloud over to the right on the horizon, and some fast-moving light, stratified smoky clouds.

All is very still – only the sound of a cat squawk in a nest in the hedge – feral cats or kittens in a nest.

6 May

Hedge garlic – Jack by the hedge – has colonized the strip of land where the spinney was outside my house. Butterflies love the pinprick white flowers – speckled woods, orange-tips and cabbage whites all flock to it.

> *Chaffinch*
>
> Like a child in the playground
> It slides down its song
> Climbs back
> And slides down again
> Hour upon hour until tea-time.

Drainpipes. We would get our mums to drainpipe our trousers for us: school trousers as much as we dared, and party trousers or jeans as much as possible without making them unwearable, or impossible to get off once on.

We used to buy corduroys from a shop in the Kilburn High Road that catered for the large Irish population there. The cords were for labourers, chocolate-brown, and built to last. Drainpiping them was a bit of a challenge.

There are sheds all over the country full of the cobwebbed wooden treasures of past craftsmen, and the things in them are of far more value than the carefully presented, perspex-boxed, interpreted items on show in our museums. Give me the dusty basement any day, or the mouldering, unattended displays of fossils or butterflies in glass cases as they always used to be in the Natural History Museum – and still are in rare museums like the one at Wakefield, where Charles Waterton's stuffed animals from his travels in South America are displayed, or at the Ipswich Museum.

I have a lost ant on my desk. It has been there for several days, wandering about in a baffled sort of way. I catch glimpses of it as it ducks out of the shadow of a coffee mug and dives under the overhang of my writing pad. Then it decides to make a break for it across five inches of open desk and shelter under my glasses case. But it's a restless soul, and no sooner has it arrived under the deep strip of shadow under the glasses case than it's off again, this time to the haven of an old copy of *Sight and Sound*, where, to my surprise, instead of burrowing under, it marches straight across an interview with the film director Monte Hellman about *Two-Lane Blacktop*, pausing on a picture of Dennis Wilson, James Taylor and Laurie Bird standing on a rock looking into a river. But this ant is never still. It's off again already, running along between the tramlines of grain in my Oregon pine desktop and disappearing under the blackness of the telephone. How does it survive? What is the secret of its never-ending energy?

I can't help it with directions, because I've no idea where it came from in the first place. I could make a guess and simply put it outside. But it is cold and rainy out there; not ant-weather at all, so it is better off in here, although I worry that I may accidentally squash it under a book, or under my elbow.

It is like a Palestinian, evicted from the Gaza Strip. It is a refugee from somewhere, frantic to go home, cut off from its family and fellow workers, going mad with loneliness. I suppose, if I'm honest, I feel some fellow feeling for it myself, cut off in book-purdah, while my friends are out there at play.

The knowledge that this tiny creature is lurking somewhere on my desk, but could be anywhere, means that I daren't move anything in case of causing an accident to it. Where is its home? What keeps it going all this time? Will it run out of energy? Should I feed it honey, as one would a bumblebee?

Cut off from its tribe, it has lost all sense of itself. It is really a part of a body in search of the rest of the body, like the tail of a lizard left twitching after amputation. An ant colony is really a single organism that is differentiated into various functions, chiefly feeding and breeding, so if one tiny component gets lost like this, it feels some imperative, some compulsion, to rejoin the rest of the ant-body.

I feel sorry for it, but I suppose there's nothing much I can do. Just when I think I'll never see it again, up it pops, doodling its imaginary trail all over my desk. If I could somehow get it to walk through ink and trace its path, it might make some sense, some pattern even, but I doubt it. It is just a wandering ant, a damned soul, condemned to eternal exile on my desk, like Philoctetes. The kind of ant you get in your pants. One of the few ants in the world whose natural enemy, the human, is actually concerned about its survival as an individual, except that the concept of individuality is completely alien to an ant.

Watching Millie pad her way carefully and silently through the vegetable garden, I forgot again about the question of the footprint – the footprint on the earth. This is the key: when we dig out a ditch or coppice some woodland, we should use hand tools as much as possible. A digger makes a deep impression on the earth, too deep. Only today I read of the clumsy killing of El Grande, the biggest eucalyptus tree in the world, by a Forestry Tasmania bulldozer. It had scraped all the earth off the roots and damaged the trunk and bark. To cap things off, they set fire to the tree for good measure.

Everywhere I went in Tasmania I saw the tracks of huge bulldozers crushing the delicate, under-storey life of the rainforest, its seabed, green and misty, in dappled shade and sunlight.

Those big trucks going in straight lines down the left-hand lane of the highway. Road-trains with a trailer and thirty tons of tree trunks, destined to be chipped, then pulped into paper. From tree to toilet paper, from *Fraxinus* to fax, from riverside to typing pool.

7th May

Everywhere this morning in the May sunshine I notice the sudden, magical growth of trees. The mulberry has just come into leaf overnight, only the beginnings, but yesterday there was no sign of anything more than the tiniest buds.

The ash arch is sending out shoots. The laid hedge of the wood is bursting into fresh green leaf. The coppiced hazels are sending out buds in the wood. Even the two ring-barked ash trees are sending out tiny shoots from their roots. This is magnificent courage and defiance. Both trees are still in leaf this year, although dying back in the lower branches. Soon, surely, they must die off at the top? They are living on residual sap. Tiny maples have sprung up everywhere under the places where the old maple used to overhang. I have laid the hedge to let in the light, and this is the explosion.

The ley lines of cowslips in the railway field are more pronounced than ever. Long mole runs of straight-line cowslips, self-seeded into the disturbed soil of the mole runs. But Richard says that ants may carry seeds on their backs. All the cowslip ley lines lead towards the giant three-foot anthill in the middle.

A couple of rabbits about, and, last night, a deer at the end of the middle field. We stood and watched each other for several minutes. I flinched first and walked home.

All morning I have been packing polythene freezer bags with peat that I dampened and filling them with apple pips from Kyrgyzstan. This is called 'breaking dormancy'. I have some trouble with the same thing myself, so I'm sympathetic with the apple pips. The fridge is full of these peaty bags filled with apple seeds or walnuts. I soaked and sieved the pips first – hawthorns too.

I moved the derelict shepherd's hut by tractor to a new place on the field near the concrete pad.

Often you get a strong sense of the tides and currents of history flowing through the works in the undercurrents of Mike Westbrook's *Piano*.

The piano is ticking away underneath it all, and, as the other players fall silent, it is revealed, the musical imagination of Westbrook, working constantly away underneath it all, the bedrock of this big sound.

Sometimes it ticks like a clock, then surges into a rolling tide and sweeps the music forward in a lyrical surge, into the new era of a piece, a fresh movement.

There is often a sense of moving from room to room of an idea or theme, as in the stanzas of a poem.

The language, words, are the basic component of jazz. The sounds of languages are constantly with us, and, as we ruminate on them in our heads, jazz plays with them, and with the rhythms and sounds, so that 'salt peanuts' or 'tutti frutti' turn into poems.

Musicians are always looking for total silence. Sebastian Rochford took us close to it in a superb diminuendo drum solo, simplicity itself, in which the entire audience held its breath as the drums, instruments of the greatest subtlety and delicacy in his hands, brought us to the threshold of audible sound, looked over the edge and then brought us back again. It was a great moment in an evening of telling moments.

Sometimes, when it gets too noisy in the country, I escape into the sheer throbbing silence of my flat in the city. I hear only the blackbird in the back gardens and, pressing my ear to the pillow at night, I hear the distant rumble of the tube trains on the Northern Line far beneath the house, heading out of Chalk Farm, uphill to Belsize Park, deep under Haverstock Hill.

9th May

Picking up Alfie is like tickling trout: you slide your hand along his belly and gently ease him off the ground before he knows it.

Today I heard swallows over the house, but didn't see them. I heard their wittering. I saw an orange-tip butterfly resting on the aubrietia on a flower, wings folded up to reveal the exquisite green-mottled whiteness of the wings.

10th May

There's a deep-sprung excitement about the English woods precisely because they are forbidden places – they're in private ownership. It's like Poland under the Iron Curtain. It was more exciting to visit them in that time because of their vibrant life, their exuberance, subverting the dour regime imposed upon them.

11th May

The ants are out on my desk again tonight, my Lilliputians. To them a pencil is a mighty tree and I have to be careful not to sweep them away accidentally.

12th May

I spent an hour and ten minutes servicing the Aga at lunchtime: taking the burner to bits and scraping out the caked carbon. The copper oil pipe leading into the base of the burner was choked with it. I used a screwdriver and drill bits to clear it.

Another cold, sunny day with a chilly east wind. I biked over to identify the intermediate dead-nettle for Betty Wells, and to see the green-winged orchids at the other end of the common.

Needled by a nettle, I come in nursing a knife and with a wet bunch of chard tucked under my arm.

I have disturbed a nest of bumblebees with my work around the dead trunk of the apple tree. How shall I make it stand upright securely? What buttresses shall I employ? Gary [Rowland] says drill the trunk and insert hazel rods, bent down and driven into the ground in an arbour round it. But how long will they retain their sprung strength?

I walked over to the badger sett just before dusk. Hard to walk into the wood silently – there's been so much growth recently in the rain. The rank vegetation hides the twigs lying in wait to crack. My overcoat gets caught in brambles. It is cold. Even more fresh diggings, but no sign of the badgers: no surprise, really, I made so much noise. I saw the back of some dis-appearing roe-deer. One hare.

Fed up with sitting inside at my desk, I went out and started up the tractors and attached a chain to the three big ash trees lying out in the long meadow. They soon would be invisible in the growing hay, and I wanted to get them on to the concrete pad where I do most of my woodwork so I could raise them on to chocks to season clear of the ground, with a free air current all round. Just climbing on to the tractor and chugging about the land was stimulating and got me thinking about the trees when they were growing tall beside the pond.

I wrapped the chains round the first trunk and dragged it behind the tractor into the home meadow and on to the concrete pad, then dragged round the other two, flailing about in the tractor's wake like dolphins.

Today, I went all round Diss trying to buy an organic chicken. Safeway doesn't sell them, and at Brown's the butcher Roger Brown said I was the first person to ask for one for years. He said he could order one in for me, but it would take several days and cost £12 for a four-pound chicken. 'Maybe I should start rearing these birds myself and sell them to you,' I said.

Goosegrass has begun to grow up so high in the flowerbed outside my study window that it is already a foot or two over the panes, like a green shutter, threatening to block out the light. Because the window faces south, the stems are backlit against the deeper green of the lawn, and I notice the tiny hairs on each stem and on the edges of leaves. I have a rough idea that the function of these hairs is to catch hold of things and give the rampant plant a leg-up as it grows. But I have to admit that I should be very interested in the science of these hairs: how they evolved, how they relate to other kinds of hairs on other plants; the whole question of plant trichology.

13th May
Early swim. Ramona [Koval] on the phone 8 a.m. All one asks of one's friends is that they remain one step ahead. To have them lagging behind risks plunging into banality.

The Mellis boys now express their joy at the coming of spring by riding little trail bikes all over the common, drowning out the lesser songs of blackcap, chiffchaff and song thrush. These fart-boxes resound across the wide surface of our inland sea of green. We have sunsets worthy of Turner to a soun ,track of sterile adolescent testosterone.

15th May

If I can be enchanted by my cat, rolling in joy on the brick terrace before me, why can't I be enchanted by a green shield bug in my vegetable garden, or two ants meeting and exchanging information with a flourish of their antennae? Or the billowing fizz of cow-parsley in full flower?

Midday. Blood-curdling screeching of foxes – probably cubs – from the hedgerow up the field through my open study window. A fox-tussle. Millie stands, or crouches, in the kitchen doorway with her ears flattened on her head. She looks at me in alarm. On the kitchen floor, a patch of fresh blood: a mystery. A field mouse? No, surely too much blood? Pale red blood, soaking into the brick and mortar of the kitchen floor.

I walk up the field to investigate. Little haloes of stamens' ruffed courtiers (as all the plantains flower, like tiny courtiers' ruffs, all bowing and nodding to each other).

Later, at 2 p.m., I notice a sudden, persistent, almost frantic buzzing at the windowpane and forsake my desk to investigate, imagining it must be a bumblebee, temporarily nobbled by an old cobweb, or tricked by the glass into exhausting itself.

What I find instead is a housefly, snagged in a spider's web and firmly in the grasp of a small house spider's fangs. The spider has the fly by its bottom and just holds on stoically, anchoring itself on a favourite old birthday card, appropriately sent to me by Claude Nuridsany and Marie Pérennou, the makers of *Microcosmos*.

For about two minutes the fly keeps up the same note with its wings, then gradually begins to tire. Then the wings cease to whirr, but the legs keep on clawing the air. One by one they fall still, until only the fly's antennae (or mouth parts) are moving. Then, when it has fallen still after seven minutes, the

111

spider makes its first move and advances over the paralysed, moribund corpse to bite into the head, presumably injecting more poison.

Now the spider is moving backwards, still gripping its prey by the head and dragging it between the twin sheets of the card into the shelter of its interior.

But the fly is too plump to fit, so the spider, now ten minutes into its kill, crawls about the corpse as if inspecting it, pauses for thought, then wheels about abruptly and disappears inside the birthday card. The fly, now apparently quite dead, remains aloft in the web.

The whole exercise has taken a quarter of an hour.

The walnut is coming suddenly into leaf, and flowering, and all the flowers are falling on the ground like green caterpillars, hawkmoth probably, and they leave a yellow dust of pollen on your fingers.

The ash is coming suddenly into leaf too – a big growth of leaf today, as it has turned much warmer and mostly sunny, with a few clouds, and a red, red sunset reflected on the pond in red stripes of cloud bands.

A sudden eruption of squealing outside in the dark and I am on the edge of my bed, staring vainly out of the open summer window into the dark. Is it moorhens? I can't tell. Silence again. Foxes are out there somewhere, terrorizing the neighbourhood.

Planners have a lot to answer for on the commons. Roof heights are all wrong now. The monster executive villas dwarf the older, vernacular language of the Suffolk houses, which all had more or less the same roof height and alignment. Planners have allowed the scale and alignment of the houses round the perimeter of commons to go out of kilter altogether. So we have lost the graceful natural proportions of vernacular building.

18th May
Worked in the vegetable garden in the evening and pricked out little seedlings of salad endive. The mustard is up and needs digging in.

Bumblebee workers of several kinds busy in the blue comfrey bells. Cherries and blackcurrants now ripening on the trees and bushes. I was woken early by Alfie with a baby moorhen in his mouth, but he dropped it on the terrace, I rushed him, and it got away into the long grass and, I hope, the moat, back to its squawking mother.

The reason Suffolk people feel so close to the sea is perhaps because to travel the landscape itself is to be at sea, navigating by a row of flint church towers, or encountering a tractor, trawling its plough across a sea of furrows with a flock of seagulls in its wake.

The skies are always beautiful.

I've seen few butterflies this year at Mellis: a couple of be-draggled orange-tips, a dozen or so limp cabbage whites, with even these beginning to be precious and rare. I've seen precisely one red admiral on the nettle patch, no peacocks on the buddleia, and no tortoiseshells or commas, and it's 18 May already.

When I used to mow the hay, the tractor radiator was plastered all over with meadow browns and hedge browns and speckled woods. Where are they now? When I walked up the seventy acres past Potash Farm, butterflies rose before me in a continuous cloud like pollen out of the grass. They were all over the deep blue flowers of the hardheads; they love knap-weed. It is as though someone has come along and swept them all up.

What does a bird hear? What does the blackbird on my lawn hear as it cocks its head to one side and listens, then picks a worm or a grub out of the soil?

Cats are angels. They sustain me invisibly by their presence. They are full of love, and they engender peace. They are house-hold angels, like the swallows in the chimney.

24th May

A walk with Andrew in Burgate Wood. First, the beauty and mystery of ancient coppiced hazels round the wood's edge. We clamber in over the ditch and up the ditch bank. It is still a deep ditch and a substantial bank, and must have been enormous in medieval times. Now it is full of nettles, enriched with the nitrogen of centuries of leaf mould. Inside the wood it is dark but quite open under the canopy of the huge old hazel and hornbeam trees. Hazels were once coppiced in the usual way, but they have been allowed to grow on for perhaps seventy or more years, since the 1920s even, and are now massive and very tall, the poles fanning outwards and leaning under their weight like vast Italian pavement restaurant parasols.

The hornbeams were at one time pollarded, often quite low, at about three feet, against rabbits and deer. They are now great twisted giants, plaited and knotted into fantastical shapes, with huge, spiralling, sinewy branches reaching up into wine-glass shapes.

Underfoot is a dark green carpet of dog's mercury, and, as we strike into the light of a ride, there are dense patches of royal-blue bugle, yellow pimpernel, stitchwort, ragged robin, herb Robert, silverweed, cuckoo flower. Also St John's wort and wild strawberry, and the woodland hawthorn. Soon we encounter a great moat enclosing the banked mound of a big earthwork, perhaps the site of a wood-framed hunting lodge in earlier times. We cross the moat at a shallow, muddy point where there are deer prints, and explore the earthwork, a big raised islanded platform some two hundred feet square that must have represented a huge expenditure of hand labour with primitive tools.

Emerging back into the wood, we went on, ducking under half-fallen branches of hazel and hornbeam and meeting superb individual ash or oak trees here and there. Some trees had holes or hollows, and we speculated about what had inhabited them.

Down the sudden vista of a ride we saw a deer. It saw us, and crashed off into the undergrowth. Then, deeper into the darkness of a big sweep of ancient hornbeams, I caught sight of a fox. It was looking straight at me and lying down. Why? It seemed to move its head, and as I unfroze and we both moved closer to it, we realized it was dead, and the movement I had seen was that of flies. It was lying across a tumulus of raised, freshly dug earth and sticks, surrounded by a circle dug deep into the wood's floor, a deep groove clawed out of the ground by the frantic animal, which had been trapped and half strangled round the waist by a wire snare tethered to an iron stake. In its efforts to escape, the fox must have tightened the noose of the wire and exhausted itself as it raced round and round the wall of death it had excavated with its torn and bloodied paws.

We left the animal with some reluctance, dragging ourselves out of the magnetic field of its all too recent suffering – it could not have been dead for more than twelve hours, and we both wished we could have come upon it sooner and somehow rescued it, probably getting bitten in the process. I imagined approaching the terrified fox and trying to reassure it. Would I have talked to it? Certainly: 'I'm not going to hurt you. Look, I have no gun.' But I would almost certainly have needed to fetch my wire cutters from home. Or would we have been able to pinion the fox between us, perhaps with a heavy branch, and somehow loosen the noose and work it off the body?

It is quite legal to use snares to kill foxes, provided they are not the free-running kind that can sever an animal in two. Leg snares are illegal; the noose must tighten over the head, although this one had somehow gripped the fox round its belly. But the law says that such snares must be inspected regularly, every day, and this one clearly had not. Perhaps it was simply that the fox had had the misfortune to get caught on a weekend. The gamekeeper was at home with his feet up, watching football.

We soon came to another moat, even wider and deeper than the one before, so we took a wide swing through the ranks of ancient hornbeams to skirt round it. More deer tracks; roe-deer, by the look of them. We swung along a wide ride on to the track that leads to Hall Farm, passing an old pollard ash tree that had completely enveloped an iron gate as it grew, so gate and tree were a single structure, and the tree itself had pleached its boughs together, giving it a buttressed, column-like appearance. The wood full of robin song but otherwise silent.

Home to tea and wine, then I worked later and slept eleven hours, from 11.30 to 10.30!

Worked on the shepherd's hut and taped up new glass into the end window. The hut needs a coat of paint and some repairing to keep it weather-proof, although it is still remarkably cosy inside, with candles in Moroccan lanterns and birds singing in the hedges all around. As I sit working at the table, I hear gentle fidgeting and squeaks of fledglings in the wall – tits, I think, that have found their way into the cavity between the boards.

Inside the hut there is a mirror, a pine bed, a small table and a chair, and a little Summerfield No. 20 iron stove in one corner near the door, with a stainless-steel pipe that sometimes glows in the dark in winter when the stove is opened up and roaring its miniature roar. There are steel plates up the walls all round the stove to reflect the heat back inside and to prevent fire. In the other corner, by the door, is a little corner cupboard with extra blankets, spare candles and matches, and warming bottles of whiskey and red wine.

The hut looks out over the middle field, now filling with yellow pools of buttercups, ox-eye daisies and the purple of vetches. Dusk is falling, and the robins are last to sing.

25th May

Today there is a frog in my woodpile in the vegetable garden. I swim two lengths in the moat. It is 15/16°C and the water is clear after recent rains. Cold, but not impossible. The ladder seems to lose another rung each year. Time, perhaps, to make a replacement. I'm also considering building a new landing deck for the front pond, to take the place of what used to be a fishing platform for the village children, before parents stopped allowing their offspring out into the countryside alone.

Longhand. The advantages of longhand, like longboat, long term, longbow. All good things, and longing too.

The short cut and the long way round. The long view. Long leg.

The idea of 'creepy-crawlies' discussed on the *Today* programme – on the TV show *I'm a Celebrity Get Me Out of Here*, someone called Phil Tufnell had eaten five plates of 'creepy-crawlies'.

These TV shows treat nature as a threat – compounding the couch-potato problem by actively alienating nature.

Why write? A writer needs a strong passion to change things, not just to reflect or report them as they are. Mine is to promote a feeling for the importance of trees through a greater understanding of them, so that people don't just think of 'trees', as they mostly do now, but of each individual tree, and each kind of tree.

Look at Richard Flanagan and his strong political campaign against Forestry Tasmania and its destruction of the old-growth forests. He has very publicly withdrawn from the literary prize sponsored by Forestry Tasmania, and he has even produced car stickers attacking the use of poison to kill marsupial animals in newly felled forests.

Walk/cycle: to far end of the common. Now two smart signs outside Pountney Hall. Nobody ever had names or signs outside their farms or houses, least of all Alice Bailey, who lived at Pountney Hall with her cats, chickens, ducks and geese all pottering in and out of the brick-floored kitchen with her. She rode a bike up and down the mile of the common to catch the bus into Diss or to Stowmarket in all weathers until well into her eighties. Nobody ever had house signs because everybody knew their neighbours anyway.

Then on to the moated mound where the windmill once stood that gave Mellis its name. The moat runs most of the way round the mound, and probably used to run all the way round. It's hard to tell now, but the northern part of it is deepest and still full of water, with woody nightshade growing in it, festooned with manes of algae. The mound used to be a mass of cow-parsley – now not nearly so much. It must have been weed-killed with a broad-leaved herb spray by the farmer who cut the hay a few years ago. It is now recovering: sorrel, cow-parsley, knapweed, lesser stitchwort, buttercup, all grow here. I think the whole of this section has been fertilized too, because the grass is unusually long and thick. It has the feel of a fertilized grass sward. Should this moat be dug out, 'cleaned' out, de-silted? Yes, I think it should. But a part of me is very glad that the windmill mound that gave the village its name isn't signposted or marked by an interpretation board or anything: that it passes unnoticed by most people, an anonymous, numinous place.

In London, in Museum Street, I find a little country spider on my rucksack. It comes crawling out and walks up the arm strap, then pauses and wonders where it is, and where to go next.

I keep finding it about my person: on my sleeve or on my jacket lapel. It stays with me somehow all the way home on the train to Suffolk and escapes on to my study desk, then out into the garden through the open window.

Richard and Ronnie, both priest-like in character: Ronnie preaching sermons, Richard preaching flowers and birds –

both wanting to communicate the sacredness of the earth. Oliver [Bernard] too, trudging to Mass with the nuns each morning at Quidenham. 'The priest-like task', 'divine landscapes', sanctified by walking.

The old tracks underlie our modern arterial system. The word 'artery' isn't right, because they are part of a more circular system of overlapping circles; each parish had people who overlapped into the next – the fishmonger, the timber-hauler.

All the friends who once came here to stay now have places of their own near by, all preoccupied by rebuilding and extending them: building brick-walled vegetable gardens or extension wings, or converting old barns with as much oak as possible. Oak represents value now and is like gold teeth here: you have an oak staircase, an oak floor, oak banisters. Yet I can't help preferring the things an earlier generation of us did on far less money – the things done on not enough money, like Tony Weston's house, with most of the barn left in its natural condition as a barn.

Poem for Frank [Crook, Roger's uncle]

A ragged kite slips sideways down the motorway
Tawny wood floor of a beech hangar
Rhododendrocide committed in the wood.
Livid green of spring beech in sunshine.
It's fifty years since I rode ponies
Or rose early to head out with a poacher's gun.
Once, we felled a squirrel.
Touching the warm, thin fur as you slotted back the gun
Into the innocent walking stick.
Yellow tulips on a roundabout
Fanned into flame by an east wind.
(Modest stillness and humility.)
A golden evening in Burnham Beeches.
You first showed me compost and its making.
We sat in the kitchen window watching jackdaws in a nest.
It is your birthday, Frank,
And Woods draw together.
Woods and Crooks have always gone together.
A springtime autumn, with the summer still to come,
To warm you in your ninetieth year,
With your nine bean-rows in a bee-loud glade.
Sea-urchin fossils along the codger's windowsill
Next to the lych gate.
You're gaining on the ninety-nine churchyard yews.
Armed with a fossil hammer,
To Painswick Quarry we went,
Past Finbar Luney at Prinknash Monastery.
We found belemnites and devil's toenails,
Ammonites and an occasional sea urchin.
The trilobite eluded us,

Questing on Haresfield Beacon
Or damming the millstream down Edge Lane.
The secret, rushing, ivy-covered derelict mill.
Ring out, wild harebells,
You'll soon reach retirement age.
Frank, now an in-law to the outlaw Woods,
Only nine fewer years than yews in Painswick Churchyard.
Crooks, outlaws, finding a natural home amongst the Woods,
Became in-laws.
Preparing for the ascent of Painswick Beacon
With a fossil hammer and a sandwich box.
It is your birthday, Frank,
In Painswick Churchyard ninety yews are garlanded for you.
Patiently, you fostered our passions:
Flowers, fossils, quarried from the beacon.
Slad, Nailsworth, Woodchester, Haresfield
Beacon, Birdlip, Pitchcombe.
A grass snake swimming a pond at Woodchester.
A mass of dandelion clocks in a meadow on the slopes
Of Painswick Beacon. Faces in a crowd – a wind farm,
Wood pasture on Cooper's Hill above Gloucester.

27th May

The hottest May Day for fifteen years they say. Moat hits boiling point at 16°C or even up to 17 or 18. I swim a few lengths, head well up, breaststroke, avoiding the odd floating algae. Water clear enough underneath but heavily dusted with pollen, clouds of it off the cow-parsley and the buttercups in the meadow, and the billowing may blossom.

Well-fed blackbirds sing better because they develop fuller throats – like busty opera singers.

Sleeping in Burgate Wood on the moated island of the old hall, I put my cheek against the loam and the cool ground ivy, and when I close my eyes I see the iceberg depths of the root-world of the wood. Walking here, picking my way through the wood, I thought of it as perpendicular, until I lay down and entered the ground-world. This is the part of a wood that only reveals itself occasionally after a big storm, when trees keel over and the roots are thrown suddenly upright, clutching earth and stones. How deep do roots go?

A radio thought: the soundtrack here, the singing of countless birds throughout my waking hours from 4 a.m., is of the utmost importance. It is actually quite noisy with birdsong here, all concentrated into a mile of hedgerows – full, wide, dense hedges like the ramparts of a castle. A kind of maze of them surrounds the little fields, and the birds love them for making nests. So there is great competition amongst all the birds for space, for a few square yards of territory, and so they sing longer and louder and more lustily. Because the surrounding fields have been made into bare-blown, featureless prairies, they flock to these hedges as an oasis of green and blessed cover for their nests, a place they can call home. And for a bird the most important aspect of household maintenance is singing. Perching as high up as you can and singing for as long and as hard as you can.

30th May
Swallows and swifts flying high above the house at last – but in transit, I think, not planning to stay. Still moody weather, sultry sunshine, lush grass in between clouds of cumulus. Cow-parsley immense. Roses coming out or budding.

June

There are definitely two different orchids in Cowpasture Meadow now: spotted orchids on the left side, halfway, and green-winged over to the right.

Dozens of cuckoo flowers at the bottom of the field: probably two hundred. Two or three elms need to be cut down and burnt because diseased. There are plenty of healthy elms thriving, and twenty to thirty feet high.

6th June
Outside my study window there are tits, a little family of four or five, all diligently pecking off the aphids on a rose. The perfect gardeners, so much better than a spray.

There was a time for us too when Suffolk and the whole of the Waveney Valley was terra incognita, like the hills, woods and ponds around Thoreau's cabin at Walden.

As Thoreau said in *Walden*, heaven is under our feet as well as over our heads.

Last night at dinner I sat between two women. The one on my right told a story about a sudden increase in the numbers of green woodpeckers in the Fens where she lives with her husband. The woodpeckers couldn't resist the clapboard walls of their house, and pecked a hole and built a nest in the cosy recesses of the insulated cavity wall while they were away on a spring holiday. They reacted with annoyance instead of delight, evicted the woodpeckers and had the wall repaired. 'It cost us £600 in new insulation and builders' bills,' she said. She complained they were forced to hang balloons all round the house from the eaves to repel the woodpeckers. I suggested it might be more rewarding to have the builders adapt the chosen section of wall into a built-in woodpecker bird-box.

The woman on my left then chimed in with a story about the swallows that would insist on nesting under the eaves of their house. (They may in fact have been house martins.) Her husband had knocked down the nest, and was obliged to put up wire netting to keep the hapless birds at bay. 'They were so messy,' she said. 'Droppings everywhere, and they were so noisy too.'

Roses just coming out fully in this first flush of heat. Up at six this morning, the sun rising through trees directly, centrally, in end-bedroom window of the house.

I lay in bed this morning, trying to think what exactly it is that a crow's call resembles. How to describe the hollow, cast-iron, metallic, mechanical ring within the crow's throat. For some reason it reminds me of Watford, and Benskin's Brewery at Croxley Green, and the viaduct the train passed over on the way to my violin lessons on Saturday mornings with Mr Piper. It makes me think of the old Albion lorries the brewery used for its deliveries of Benskin's brown ale, and the sound of their starter motors. That could be it, the special quality of sound of a starter motor that hasn't quite engaged the under-note; the abrasive call is so haunting precisely because it is so hard to pin down, so defiant of description.

I never wanted to be at those violin lessons; I wanted to be with my friends gathered on bicycles outside Giles Record Shop in the middle of Hatch End. I can remember the real thrill and conviction of going up to the counter at Giles and buying Buddy Holly's 45 with 'Peggy Sue' on one side and 'Everyday' on the other the moment it came out. Or buying Sidney Bechet beside my friend Ian Keynes, who boldly demanded 'Anything by Dizzy Gillespie', putting the accent on 'Gil' and eliding the 'es'.

The great antidote to racism is travel. If only people would travel more adventurously, they would soon learn the deep respect for other peoples and cultures of the true traveller.

I don't mean tourist but traveller: one who finds himself depending on the goodwill and hospitality of other people – the natural human civility of other people in other countries – and who knows what it is to be a foreigner.

Building the new table top at Mellis in the study. Perfectionism kicks in, and all the same self-critical criteria that go into a piece of writing. I make a yew bracket to fix to the oak beam and support the top, and a careful wooden subframe or chassis. I fill the grain with Polyfilla and carefully stain it pale blue with a tiny paintbrush. In one of the holes in the top I shall set a watch face, or a smooth round pebble from the beach.

I slept in the shepherd's hut last night after an eight-length evening swim in the moat, now beginning to weed up – a beautiful, nearly full moonlit night. Very bright, hardly proper darkness at all. At ten to four I was woken up by a warbler (not sure which) hopping along the tin roof of the hut, then striking up the most beautiful song, at first utterly solo in the half-light, soon joined by other birds. It sang its heart out, moving about the roof now and again between phrases or cadenzas to a new vantage point. Easing myself up on one elbow about twenty past four, I inched back the curtain and surveyed the field. Yellow pools of buttercups, and here and there a pyramidal orchid, and even a lovely lush marsh orchid in intense purple and with a huge stack of a flower like a wedding cake.

A crow was flying in big circles about the field, climbing steeply now and then, then gliding down, as if for pure pleasure. I dozed back to sleep but was awoken by a most terrific rumbling and shaking of the whole hut, and a scratching sound. I thought a cat must somehow have leapt in through an open window and on to my bed. But I think it was the roe-deer, the one with the faun, rubbing against the hut, as I heard what sounded like hooves disappearing through the long grass. The birdsong now far too raucous for sleep, so I adjourned to the house over dewy grass for breakfast, and to wrap a leaving present for Frank Gooderham, my lovely postman.

I found myself in tears as I wrote his card, inscribed a copy of my book for him and wrapped the present: a bottle of Graham's port, the book and an audiotape, and my card. I hadn't fully realized, until that point, how deeply important he has been to me: working and living here alone for so long, I looked forward each morning to the cheering flash of his red van through the trees, tuning my ears for the hum of its Ford engine as it approached and changed gear along the common and down my bumpy track.

He arrived in his van for the last time at about twelve o'clock, and when he handed over the mail to me it was all either of us could do to even speak, both choking back the tears. I shall miss him terribly.

A chiffchaff lustily singing in the garden all morning, sunshine, pigeons cooing, warblers, all the roses are out. A call from Richard, who has discovered a lane, Darrow Lane, near his house, with sulphur clover, meadow vetchling, bee orchid and hoary plantain, all growing happily.

How much better to scythe down one's grasses after having allowed them to reach their full height and flowering glory. People forget that grasses are flowers, and magnificent graceful things too, that will dry and preserve themselves in winter.

How much quieter and more contemplative to scythe than to mow with a machine, and how much better to make a haystack on the spot, a roofed house out of which all the insects, beetles and grubs can crawl back on to the lawn and resume their lives, perhaps in some neighbouring bit of cover.

After scything and working up a sweat, a long swim in the moat; cleared out the Canadian pondweed, hugging armfuls of it to my breast and breaststroking one-armed to the bank.

Drove up the M1 to see Richard at St Andrew's Hospital, Northampton, a lovely pale sandstone Palladian house where John Clare lived for years to the end of his life.

Richard and I sat in the sun on the terrace and looked out across acres of mown grass and park trees. Big, mature acacias, cedars, sycamores, copper beeches. The sycamore was also copper, from the red pigment you see in the leaf veins. As we sat there, from 3.20 p.m. until 6.00 p.m., different shifts of birds came and went, feeding on the lawn: first a half dozen blackbirds, then wood pigeons, then a pair of crows, a wagtail, then magpies, etc. A hen sparrowhawk had been hunting up above too. Then out came the rabbits, dozens of them all over the lawns outside the hospital, all very tame. Richard had watched one roll in the grass on its back like a cat the day before.

There are foxes and badgers, and no doubt hedgehogs.

Richard talked with enthusiasm about the great reed-bed at Peterborough and the plan by the RSPB, which has already created another at Lakenheath.

He also spoke of an invention for the study of the canopies of rainforests: a kind of giant jellyfish, inflatable, on which scientists can walk about and study the canopy, having been dropped on to it by helicopter. They discovered 'leaf shyness' or 'top-leaf shyness', in which the leaves all grow apart from each other, seeking light, but also sharing it.

I told Richard about the Wollemi Pine and its discovery near Sydney in a gorge in the Blue Mountains only be reached by abseiling in.

Richard spoke of the possibility of creating at least two riverine forests soon, and how two East Anglian estuaries were being considered. Sallows, willows, alders, etc. Cuttings would establish them very quickly.

We talked of the long root systems of figs, and of the fig forest on the Don at Sheffield, where an interesting flora has developed: three different kinds of balsam, tansies and bluebells, washed down from the Pennines.

The root of a fig at Magdalen College, Oxford, reached through into the cellar and planted itself in a bottle of port.

I spoke of the fig tree at Manaccan, and Richard said the fig has very long roots that could travel down inside the hollow of a wall and find moisture in the ground.

Every now and again you find yourself slipping into a little pocket, a little envelope, of country that is unknown to anyone else, which feels as though it is your own secret land.

I got up at 4.30 a.m. and went over to Wortham Long Green to look for orchids, etc., and especially the dyer's greenwood. Followed Richard's directions saying that it was at the far end of the green, but couldn't find it at all. Did find yellow bedstraw (lady's) and the white heath bedstraw, and knapweed, self-heal and a marsh orchid. Ox-eye daisies too.

In other parts I found marjoram, meadow cranesbill in the verge, two or three feral cardoons, forget-me-not, a big stand of dozens of marsh orchids at the other end, near the T-junction, bee orchids next to more marsh orchids, hay rattle at the end near the tennis courts, hoary ragwort and the gnarled old pollarded trunk of the black poplar, still just about alive with a single surviving branch. I have seen others on this common deliberately set on fire up their hollow trunks, which act as chimneys.

I went down to Redgrave Church, on its hill above the corn-fields, and stumbled upon the grave of Julie Ward. It was a shock, realizing I was standing before the grave of a young woman who had been murdered in 1988 in the Kenyan bush, her body mutilated and half burnt, and her murderer relentlessly pursued by her grieving father, outraged at Kenyan corruption and laziness.

Julie Ward was a talented photographer and had taken some fine pictures on her African travels. It is obvious from the photographs that she was courageous and adventurous. The simple square headstone bore an engraving of a hippopotamus above her name. The animal stands on the savannah plains of Kenya, with a few sparse trees in the background. I hadn't expected to find a hippo amongst the rabbits and moles of Redgrave Churchyard. But why Redgrave? It was good to think that the young woman had been buried here in this beautiful, isolated place, overlooking the African-looking bleached cornfields from high up.

Redgrave's plague history lurks under the glacial hill on which the church stands, giving the impression of thousands of victims. As Oliver Rackham remarks, there are, if you reckon it up, ten thousand bodies buried beneath every English village churchyard. With its air of solitude and isolation, and *elevation*, Redgrave graveyard hovers above the surrounding countryside, looking across to Redgrave Fen, and begins to conform to Thoreau's idea that graves should bear the legend 'Here rises', not 'Here lies', the soul of *x* or *y*. Graves, he thinks, should be starry-pointing.

Robins are the angels of my vegetable garden. You turn round and they're not there. Then there they are, next to you.

If you want to know what it's like to be a tree, sleep with a cat on your bed and feel it manoeuvring and exploring your curves and hollows for the most comfortable nest.

Yesterday, I put on shorts and a pair of waders and waded into the front pond to drag out the dead branches left there after the razing of the spinney. I tied a rope to the garden rake and lassoed a big limb of ash that had lain in the pond like Excalibur for months, reaching out of the black pond as if beckoning, beseeching rescue. I leant on the rope and towed it out, ever so slowly, and, as it rose from the water, it dripped like a breaching whale and glistened silver with fish spawn.

I mined dark orange clay from a small pond edge where tadpoles were crowding in a wriggling mass, and barrowed it round to my dam at the neck of the front pond. The water level had been dropped too low by the digger-man, who didn't understand that the system of ponds on the common is meant to collect water, not to drain it away.

The signs are all there for anyone to read if they want to: 'Cowpasture Farm', 'Cowpasture Lane'. The twenty-four ponds on the common were reservoirs for the long, hot summers of grazing. The trees were there for shade. The seventy acres of furze were for fuel for firing the bread ovens, and the moats were to keep the cattle off the arable land, away from the corn.

Grandpa Wood – cracking open the coal to show me fossil ferns, the concealed history of the carboniferous forest.

Trees make time stand still.

Hands and trees, hands and wood.

24th June

Midsummer Day. The perfect morning for it. Wood pigeons cooing in the young elms, and ashes surrounding the garden in deep shadow. Spider's gossamer threads glinting in the sunshine. Robins on the lawn. There's a goat-beard head stuck in a jam jar swivelling in the breeze at the open window of my study. An earwig explores the window frame, and an ichneumon fly elegantly strolls up and down the windowpane. A distant cockerel across the field, and even the neighbour's distant barking dogs, or Michael's crop-scarer across the common, sound benign this morning.

Yesterday I stood by the front pond and watched a carp slowly emerging from the black depths, rising imperceptibly by slow degrees until I could see its face, and its eyes, and its great gaping, gulping mouth, and then, as it caught the sun, its golden scales. I calculated that it must be at least twenty-five or even thirty years old and was one of the fish Barry Day deftly caught in his digger bucket when he was removing the silt from the moat fifteen or eighteen years ago.

A willow warbler sings in the spinney by the old goat sheds. Bumblebee workers, all from same colony, gather pollen and nectar from the new deep crimson flowers of the water fig-wort. Great three- and four-foot spires of elegant little flowers of the most amazing deep crimson. I record them, and the post van arriving too.

Anarchy reigns on this green and yet it works well enough in its way and still produces some spectacular flowers.

Today my task is to scythe down the cow-parsley that billowed in waves of white lace before my window until last weekend. Now I have to cut it before it seeds.

The scythe – sharpened on the whetstone from the River Usk.

And later on I must make two croquet mallets for Terence on my lathe. And attend to the tree nursery – weed it, and weed the felled spinney of nettles.

At about 5 p.m. I go out and begin scything the cow-parsley in the garden outside my study facing the common. Its flowering is over, and it is going to seed. I need a new scythe blade, really, but they're getting harder to find. I shall buy one in Chagford next time I'm on Dartmoor.

Working with a scythe is silent, rhythmical and conducive to thinking. A power tool simply jams the brain solid with its din and violence and sense of hurry. A scythe is unhurried, but it can fell a fair-sized area of grass and herbs in an hour of steady work, and by six I have very nearly cleared the whole front lawn.

Now I fetch the pitchfork and rake all the cut cow-parsley and long grass into compact heaps and carry each one to a bigger haycock in the middle of the lawn. As it grows higher into a cottage-loaf shape, it becomes springier, and bounces a little each time a new load is dropped on the top. It will soon settle, especially when it begins to heat up inside and compost.

This is my idea: to make a pile of the cut stems on the lawn and let it compost down, thus reducing its weight and bulk to something more manageable for eventual carting to the vegetable garden.

As I work all the robins in the neighbourhood gather on the cut grass and begin feeding and hunting for flies. Then both cats come and sit in the new-mown hay, observing the robins with feigned indifference. All of them are following deep instincts, attracted by the smell of the hay, the sounds of me working and the smells of fresh-cut herbs.

On my daily bike ride later on, I had stopped outside Gislingham, opposite a small wood and a pile of blue cartridge shells, to satisfy my curiosity about an unlikely plant community growing along a high field bank where the road has become a hollow-way on the descent into Gislingham. The ditch was dug much deeper along here two or three years ago, and the fields were drained. Growing in the ditch and on the bank are: fool's watercress, water figwort, tufted vetch, common yellow vetch, cornflowers, whose seed must have already been in the ground, meadowsweet.

I was sitting on my bike admiring all this when I heard the rumble of hooves thundering lightly up the road in my direction. I looked round and there was a pair of roe-deer galloping straight up the middle of the road towards me. They saw me and veered off into the cornfields, one bounding off one way, the other off to the far side of the road. Both were hinds, and probably had fauns hidden up somewhere, perhaps in the shooting wood. Deer move through fields of corn like dolphins through the sea.

Tomatoes on toast was about the only thing my father knew how to cook, and when my mum was away we would eat the dish for breakfast and dinner too, with toast and dripping for lunch. I used to love arranging the halved grilled tomatoes on the toast like jellyfish.

Cats are, as Norman O. Brown says in *Life Against Death*, 'polymorphously perverse'. That is to say they are gloriously alive in every part of their body and get equal pleasure from the stimulation of any part of it, free of what Brown calls 'the tyranny of the genitals'.

This morning Alphonse lies on the bare earth outside the front of the house full length on his back, stretching and rolling from side to side or raising all four legs into the air and just lying on his back. He purrs to himself and gives that cat-smile by narrowing his eyes when he looks across at me.

Cheltenham. A walk with Steve [Ashley] from the top of Cleeve Hill, where the road crosses over the crest. We went up a green lane past a field where I once slept and was disturbed by police at 2 a.m. Wind blowing ash trees and exposing the pale undersides of all the leaves, silver flash, vulnerable, like pale leg skin. Steve says willow leaves look cold and white blown from underneath, blown back to front. The tree turned inside out, caught unawares. A whitebeam stands out.

Steve talks of 'Lord Randall' and the 'Babes in the Wood' – folksong stories of dark deeds in woods: infanticide with a penknife that won't wipe clean of blood, but spreads more and more of it all over the wood. Green turning to red.

We walk down the track, turn left into a field and come to a stop at a farmyard – derelict barns, roofs teetering on fractured stone walls half crumbled and collapsed, and an oozing midden of cow muck in the yard. A dead stop, and somehow symbolic as we turn tail and walk back. 'Comeuppance Farm', we call it.

I sleep beside Steve's paper birch, the only stately paper birch in Cheltenham.

Laugharne. Here's a classic case of the Heritage Industry getting its dead hand on a wild place and taming it to death. [Iain] Sinclair and his A13 and celebration of the Beckton Alp is a necessary antidote to all this. Dylan Thomas's Boathouse, brown-signed from the M4. Tarmac all the way, even on the path along the steep shore of the huge estuary to the garage.

You arrive in Laugharne, go past a wooden hut with a cowboy on horseback painted on the door, and up to where a path branches off the road by Julianne's Uni-Sex Hair Salon; past the Three Mariners and the graveyard where Thomas is buried under a mound of fresh flowers. Brown's Hotel, where he drank, is down the street.

Thomas mostly wrote not in the boathouse but in its wooden garage. So, like garage music, his was garage poetry. I see straight away that it has the optimum dimensions for a writing shed: fourteen feet by nine, with a whitewashed boarded ceiling over a pair of pine cross-beams a foot above head height.

There are two windows in the shed, now brought up to a standard of repair far higher, I imagine, than in Thomas's day, and a wooden floor with a single diminutive scrap of a rug on it.

The place has been window-dressed to look as if the famed artisan has just popped out in mid-flow for a cup of tea, or more likely a beer or a pee. One imagines that DT must have been a much stained man: his fingers nicotine-stained, and perhaps his trousers eroded by dribbled pee in the frequent visits to the gents at Brown's or the Three Mariners.

The shed, or garage, has a wood-stove on one wall, wooden kitchen table by the window that faces south out on to the estuary and miles of mud flats, and two simple slat-backed wooden chairs, one with the poet's jacket half slung over it. Balls of screwed-up paper litter the floor, perhaps drunkenly misaimed at the waste-paper basket, which overflows with failed stabs at 'Do Not Go Gentle into that Good Night' or 'The force that through the green fuse drives the flower'. These days, he would simply have pressed the 'delete' button.

The waste paper would have constituted a serious fire risk once the stove was under way.

Around the pine-boarded walls a little gallery of pin-ups is displayed. Yeats, Lawrence, Joyce and Thomas himself, as painted by Augustus John, are all featured. On the desk, an exercise book lies open and the manuscript of a poem, scrawled with plenty of crossings out, is displayed, also an inkwell and blotting paper. For some reason the expression 'blotting his copybook' comes to mind.

The barking of a heron across the estuary and the tide surging out down a snaking mud channel. Boats lying beached on the mud on their side. A sweet chestnut spreads over the garage roof from the garden beside the path on the opposite side. Tin roof.

The wooden garage doors padlocked and a peephole, courtesy of English Heritage, allows us to peer in at the scene, like some person from Porlock stalking the great poet.

Dylan Thomas put himself on the edge of the known world, in this minimal space, looking out across the estuary, about as far away from human civilization as possible.

And if he wasn't leaving it that way, he was leaving it down the alcohol route at the bar of Brown's Hotel in the village, or down the dream route.

Cornwall – Falmouth – the Maritime Museum Boat Store. I liked the boat store best, because there were so many boats there all under polythene dust sheets, which we lifted up, and then went clambering about under a forest of spars and beams supporting still more wooden boats.

I liked the old wooden Rothschild being restored bit by bit in the shed. They stripped down the two Perkins diesel engines and cleaned every part and painted the cases green. Boats are often altered insensitively, and it takes a shipwright's eye to recognize what the boat once was and to bring it back into its natural shape.

If sailing boats were invented now, they would be either hailed or written off as some quaint form of alternative energy, a green alternative to the powerboat.

The *sets of oars* are crucial to pure sailing boats, in lieu of an engine, to get them out of trouble.

The skills of sailing these boats, with their older rigs, are disappearing, as are the skills to make them.

The Greenbank Hotel at Falmouth. Ghostliness of the waiters – 'Would sir prefer a fish knife and fork? – or of the poached talbot – tasteless, on a tasteless 'bed of fennel' – or of the 'seared Falmouth squid with tempura prawns' – only a single prawn and a handful of squid slices. Woken by seagulls above my window at 4 a.m.

The deserted house and grassy quay at Restronguet, on

my walk along the shoreline from the pub (Pandora) into Tregonwith Wood. Lapping sounds of water. Deep turquoise water beneath hanging woods.

Ralph Bird's workshop with the souped-up VW Beetle at one end and the jig for the gig keel running its length. I wondered how he gets the boats in and out – diagonally through double door at one end, perhaps.

Old boats riding off the Devoran Quay in the Carnon. Used to be a big harbour and deep-water quay here, but silted up by the mines of tin and copper.

The Cob Course. Jackie Abey lives at Burrow Farm, a long, thatched Devon farmhouse built of cob with a rambling range of barns outside. We all met in the dairy and looked at cob tiles – floor and wall – made by Jackie and Jill [Smallcombe] and varnished with linseed oil and beeswax. By varying the earth source they made tiles in different colours. Earth varies in colour often within a few hundred yards. Allow for shrinkage when you make a tile.

We all went out into the concrete-pad farmyard, where several piles of different-coloured earth sat under tarpaulins. One of deep red Devon earth, another of pale yellow ochre. Jill and Jackie often use them in strata to create coloured variety in their buildings or sculptures.

We scattered straw from a bale in a long line (one small straw bale to one ton of earth), heaped earth on top of it, turned it from either side with long straw forks, then jumped on top and trod on the mix. We barrowed it to the foundations of a circular garden shelter and laid a first 'lift' of cob on to the stone foundation and left it to dry.

Back in the dairy, we made cob bricks in 4" × 2" frames hinged with canvas or steel, 4" × 6" × 12". You turn out the bricks to dry on a pallet – keep air circulating. (Brick mix bashed in with a small mallet.)

We then began work on the bread oven. A 3'6"-diameter brick foundation, infilled with gravel and shale. On top, we placed cob bricks in a rosette and infilled with cob mixture, which we bashed in with a mallet, and then a 2" layer on top of that, flattened with a cricket bat. We also stood on top and trod in the mix, so all the time the cob is being mixed, turned and worked. On up to 2'6" level or 3 ft. Then we corbelled in the dome, leaving a doorway at the front and 4" chimney at the top.

We fired it up, and, as the fire burnt, the water came trickling and sweating out of the damp clay, and the interior began to blacken, with pale grey streaks as it heated up.

The journey home includes arriving at 6 p.m. at Liverpool Street from Bristol via Paddington and finding thousands of commuters staring at a display of departure boards that all say only one word: CANCELLED. There is almost total silence amongst the people: no one talks to each other, only into their mobiles. Everything is happening in the private sphere; they have all withdrawn from the public sphere, faced with a crisis. This is pure George Orwell *1984*, and it is exactly how it will be when a really big crisis hits London, like a major terrorist attack. People will be talking into their mobile phones to folks back home, or their friends. The idea of public engagement, of spontaneous dialogue with your neighbour, has almost ceased to exist.

And so it is in the train itself: everyone talking like mad, but apparently to themselves, not to each other. I can't face the crowds cramming on to the 6.30 train, so pause in St Botolph's Churchyard and wait for Min [Cooper], who comes over and we sit on a bench for a while, then go for a Filet-O-Fish at the McDonald's, prior to my boarding a Trainful-O-Sardines at 8.30 p.m. There is standing room only, and we eventually leave at 9 p.m. and reach Diss at 11 p.m. Eight hours from Bristol! 3 p.m. to 11 p.m.

Note: On my way to Bristol, crossing London by the Central Line, I notice the wooden banister rails at Paddington and Baker Street stations: the worn mahogany must have lost at least a quarter inch in wear, sandpapered by generations of Londoners' hands. The rails give a warm, friendly feeling to these otherwise dark, slightly threatening stations, all stairways and dark tunnels, and asphalt floors.

Now, when everyone wants to travel everywhere and do everything from pottery to writing, trees stand for rootedness. They stay in one place, and we return to them.

28th June

The middle field is like a painting just now, an Impressionist, Pointillist painting. Looking out from the shepherd's hut window there are pools of pink grasses, pools of yellow butter-cups, pools of deep green sedges, and the spires of orchids visible here and there, or the dark blue of self-heal, or the white dots of ox-eye daisies.

I am standing in the ash tunnel, which is now in full growth, or regrowth, again. The sun is filtered through chlorophyll into the green shade of the tunnel interior – the leaves are like green sunglasses, filtering sunlight and UV. When I pleach the ash tree, I have to wound it, and the tree fights back from the wound and forms a callous to heal itself, and the callous grows, cells divide, and it becomes the point of union between two trees, or even three at a time. Over time, these joints become stronger, and the cambium of one tree, and thus its xylem and phloem, begins to grow into another, until the trees are no longer separate organisms but a single being with shared sap and circu-

lation. There are no longer eight separate trees but a single one.
   The average family throws out six trees of paper a year!

My grandfather literally *came up* out of the mine and climbed on
to the higher level of time-keeping clerk; he then rose still
further by becoming a civil servant. His *rise* was through the
class or status system, and the metaphor was his elevation from
the social depths of the Walsall and Rugeley Mine.
   (Joe Deakin [Roger's great-uncle] also was *freed* to a degree
through his incarceration in Parkhurst. Paradox reigns.)

I indulge my cat – I let her loll all over my notebook, creasing
the pages outrageously as she purrs. Because she blesses the
page by her complete disregard for literature, so has she completely achieved the present.

> Bib of white, and four white feet,
> Forepaws curled in repose
> Your gloves are on.
> Now an interruption of the reverie
> To attend to some whim of grooming.
> Blessing my words with your bliss,
> Mistress of simple pleasures.

Dainty dancer and disrespecter of
Kitchen surfaces, skip from floor
To breakfast table to work table
To chest of drawers beside the window,
And we both peer
At nature in the garden.

I have always felt a special allegiance to the skylark, because it gave its name to the first magazine ever to publish my work: our school magazine. Whoever named it must have had in mind that the bird, as it soars and sings, spreads joy and hope everywhere. Recently, the numbers of skylarks have taken a steep dive, and the very mention of the bird, even its song, brings on in me a sense of deep gloom and anxiety about the fate of the wild. There is something pathetic about the few skylarks.

My very earliest memories are of lying as a baby, underneath leaves with sunlight filtering through because my mother believed that leaves filtered sunlight, allowing the most beneficial of its rays to pass through and nourish me with Vitamin

D. 'Brown as a berry' was the expression she used to describe the desired effect on my tiny body.

With plants and trees in woods abroad – say, Kyrgyzstan – I had the feeling you get when you're in a late-night bus, and you encounter a group of friends you don't know at all – total strangers – and think you would like to know them; you feel some immediate sense of kinship, that they are 'your sort'. It is like falling in love with a whole group of people at once.

Later, once you've got to know them by talking, you introduce yourselves (cf. Kavanagh's poem 'We were in love before we were introduced'). And it is love.

I can't bear to mow my lawn because it would mean mowing all the blueness out of it, the vanishing blues of self-heal, bugle and germander speedwell. They are worth more to me than the neatness of a mown lawn; in truth, I have loathed neatness ever since school – and uniform, and collars and ties, and haircuts.

A gentle tinkling as the lantern brushes against the ball grass-tops on my way across the hay meadow to the railway wagon at midnight. The dancing shadows in the grass. The deeper darkness inside the wagon.

July.

Both cats have their special places in the house: particular haunts where they curl up, inside or out in the garden or the fields.

Millie favours the shelf behind the Aga, or on top of the amplifier on my hi-fi. Alfie makes a beeline for an old cane chair at the kitchen table, or a rug over a big leather sofa that once stood in the Garrick Club.

Out on the lawn, Alfie has a nest in the long grass, now a perfectly round hollow, and Millie occupies the car bonnet or the iron manhole cover.

5th July

Last night, at a quarter past midnight, I was woken by the fox barking continuously, remorselessly, just the other side of the moat in the moat meadow. I could just hear another fox replying in a distant field, or perhaps in Thornham Wood. No sign of tracks this morning. I find that in the recent rain the seed pods of the common vetch have all burst open, revealing what I at first glance took to be jay feathers, but found were the striped insides of the seed pods. They curl open in a spiral and spin the seeds away. Hence the circular pools of vetches in the meadows.

I encourage them because of their beauty, but also because they fix nitrogen back into the soil through nodules of bacteria that form on their roots. The bacteria are nitrogen-fixing organisms that take the nitrogen from the air and put it in the soil.

I wear brown corduroy trousers: the nearest thing to the bark of a tree, just short of an out-and-out suit of Lincoln green.

6th July
Last night I went into Barn Meadow and picked the seed pods of tufted vetch for Terence and Angela [Sykes] for half an hour. I put them in a brown paper bag and left it on the kitchen table and could hear the pods exploding as they dried

out in the warm of the kitchen. I left some on my desk and the same thing happened.

The twisted pods of tufted vetch on a white sheet of paper on my desk – they twist more as they dry.

Blackcaps on the roses this morning early. I seem to be one big bruise just now – a huge nine-inch bruise on my thigh where I fell down the barn steps.

I'm standing in the home meadow in the long grass, listening to the vetch pods cracking open in the sunlight and warmth after a rainy night. The rain has softened them, then the sun has blackened and hardened them, and the stresses in the cells have caused the pods to snap open like little springs and fling out the seeds as they twist into a spiral.

Everything is going to seed now, including the orchids, and the butterflies have emerged and are flying all over the meadows. Meadow browns, ringlets (lots of them) and commas. Also red admiral and cabbage white, common blue and tortoiseshell. Orange-tips flew earlier. By now there are more meadow browns than ringlets – the reverse of last week's position.

Long grass is more mysterious than mown grass. You could be looking straight at a skylark's nest or a field mouse, a frog or a dormouse nest, and not know it. It is a jungle in miniature.

I really do want people to come home to a real fire. A nation without the flames of a fire in the hearth, and birds singing outside the open window, has lost its soul. To have an ancient carboniferous forest brought to life at the centre of your home, its flames budding and shooting up like young trees, is a work of magic.

8th July

Sunny morning after rain. I find a *pale blue* self-heal in Cow-pasture Meadow. Thistles are in flower, and bees setting up a real hum in the pools of white clover.

I pick the blackened pods of creeping vetch and crack them open to release the seed, which I sow in the hedge.

4 p.m. A flower bramble. A bramble in full flower is a great joy to see. The bramble I'm observing is in one corner of my garden, and its flowers are pale pink. It belongs to the tribe of silver-backed leaves, and the joy of it is the great multitude of insects it attracts. There's a party, a feast, going on here.

Dozens of butterflies skip about from flower to flower. Apart from the occasional comma, they are all meadow browns and ringlets. The ringlets, dusky-winged and eyed around the borders, open and shut their wings as if to wink. Bumblebees and hoverflies of every kind are humming and busying themselves from flower to flower, the bees rummaging amongst the stamens at a great rate, working with urgent efficiency. The whole bramble bush hums and pulsates with its insects. Behind it, in the denseness of the hedge, a pair of blackbirds fret and cluck over my presence. The coquettish ringlets hardly open their wings except to fly, folding them tightly shut the second they land, only occasionally relaxing them in the ecstasy of nectar.

A tiny spider drops out of the leaves and walks purposefully across my page. Not one of these insects wastes a moment on squabbling over a flower or jostling for position; instead there's a kind of dance as each forager gives way to the other. 'After you', they seem to say. A blackcap sings sweetly somewhere offstage. And the infuriating, unhappy, neurotic dogs across the field, cooped up in a cage all day, bark incessantly, miserably.

The six eyes of the ringlet and the single eye of the meadow brown are all camouflage, like the fearsome-looking black and yellow stripes of the hoverflies, mimicking the wasps that should be on this blossom too, but aren't. Wasps have become a rarity round here. Only hornets are relatively plentiful. Some of the hoverflies even gyrate their abdomens sexily, as if itching to sting. I spot hive bees and at least three or four different kinds of bumblebee.

All along the hedges of Cowpasture Meadow I hear chiff-chaffs, grasshoppers in the field, wind in the tops of the ash, elm and crab apples.

The shed where the foxes live is completely hidden by a towering bramble, a castle really, animated all over this afternoon in the sunshine by butterflies, bees and hoverflies feasting and ravishing its recently opened pink blossom.

Within each flower, in the *exploding crown* of stamens at the centre of its five pink petals, is a little colony of tiny black shiny beetles, pollen beetles, all busy feeding themselves stupid, their iridescent wing cases glinting blue, green and purple-black in the sun. All round each open flower a dozen more buds are balled up in tight fists, ready to open any day now. The foxes are probably asleep inside this citadel, for all I know.

Foxes love to lie out on patches of soft sheep's fescue (*Festuca ovina*). A long-bodied ichneumon fly explores the bramble patch. Sturdy green seed pods of bee orchids. Bundled webs full of infant spiders.

It is a Saturday afternoon, and because it's so dull I'm working in my study with the lights on. I have just written the word 'dragonfly' in my e-mail to Rob Macfarlane. (Not enough of them to eat the horseflies. An emperor dragonfly can eat 2,000 flies a day.) A moment later, a real emperor dragonfly sails into the room, buzzes right round it and approaches the light. I switch it off, and the dragonfly zooms out again.

I'm not lonely here because I feel so connected to the trees, the house, the meadows, the birds, the insects. I also feel connected to my friends. But I believe that so many people are so cut off from all the other things, the trees, etc., that it is good to make a small compensating gesture in my life and relate to them if I can.

I was seventeen when a policeman came to our door and told me my father was dead. Well, actually what happened was that my father didn't come home on his usual train and my mother was already worried, pacing the kitchen, filling the house with foreboding.

The policeman said, 'May I come in?' There were two of them, for solidarity, I suppose, on a difficult mission. My father had been found, dead, on a Bakerloo Line tube train at Euston Square Station. He died less than a mile from where my great-uncle Joe had been arrested in the Tottenham Court Road in 1892. Both policemen took off their helmets and turned them round and round by the brim as they spoke. Their overwhelming dark blue bulk filled the sitting room of our tiny bungalow, displacing something, making my mother and me feel very small and insignificant. I was sent to identify the body at the coroner's office across the churchyard of the little church at St Pancras behind the station. When I got there, the kindly coroner's assistant spared me the experience, so I never saw my father dead. He just went out that morning and disappeared out of my life. It felt odd, as well as sad. After a couple of days at home making awkward efforts to support my mother, I returned to school still wearing a black armband, as people did in 1960, and my embarrassed friends avoided my eye. It was almost as though I myself had died, so ghostly, so invisible, did I feel.

Thus did I acquire my sense of loss – a deep-seated feeling that has followed me around all my life and that I've never shaken off.

Last Sunday I counted twenty angels in the roof of Southwold Church and thought today of Skelton's 'Ware the Hawk', and how the rector caught one of his flock flying his hawk in the rafters of his church, amongst the angels and the Green Men.

Driving home from Southwold, I passed four live hedgehogs and one dead one, just killed on the road. I stopped to let one pass, switching off my lights to prevent its being dazzled. Two or three hares too, along the road from Bramfield to Walpole, eyes extra big at night, loping into the darkness.

The amazing hedge along the road that runs direct from Walpole to Blyford like a railway narrow-gauge line, which cuts into the bank of the Blythe River in its headwaters. Stunning mix of elm, oak, holly, hornbeam, like a wine glass flattened, like a plant pressed in a book, from years of hedge-laying.

We mutilate these trees and still they come back looking ever more beautiful.

The elms are returning everywhere – and ancient oaks on the lanes around Foals Green. Yellow bedstraw, agrimony, purple loosestrife, rosebay willowherb, in all the hedgerow banks.

10th July

Last night I watched a newt trekking across the rugs on my study floor, pausing now and again, as if playing Grandmother's Footsteps, freezing in mid-stride, poised. It crawled in a straight line, and I left it alone: it seemed to know what it was doing. It is only just July, but the newts are already out of the water and taking up winter quarters. The nights are getting shorter. The newt is a realist.

My house was once an acorn.

It is the hottest night of the year so far, and I sit here in my study with the door and all the windows thrown open to the garden. It is 10 p.m. and darkness has just fallen, yet hardly a moth or beetle flies in towards the bright lights on my desk. Twenty years ago there would have been hordes of them. Is it too early for crickets? Perhaps it is, but there is a silence outside that I don't seem to recognize as I look 'out into the surrounding night of nature', as Platonov says.

Rufus and Emily [Deakin, Roger's daughter-in-law] drove over from Bristol. Rufus and I walked out over the common close to the house in the evening after the hay had been turned and baled.

Magpies and crows flew up as we appeared, and we found dead and dying frogs, and live ones too, jumping towards the perimeter of the common. Also dozens of froglets, and toadlets all hopping in the grass, suddenly exposed and very vulnerable.

Black slugs, rather smart ones with fluted abdomens, were gliding about on the hay left over on the grass stubs.

If the grass-cutters hadn't been set so close to the ground, fewer frogs would have been killed.

All this shows how important the line of trees is in keeping the sun off that part of the common and keeping it damp for amphibians.

I've put some waterweed and duckweed from the moat into my al fresco outside bath, and I'm observing the water creatures in it. It's surprising how sprightly the water snails are, almost skipping about between fragments of duckweed as they feed on little microbes of algae.

12th July

The Give and Take Lawn – mow round circles of white clover for the bees. In a single disc of clover ten feet wide, at least a dozen to twenty bumblebees, nearly all orange-bummed *Bombus lapidarius*, working in the sunshine.

I have been cat-scratched so many times by brambles that I ought to hate them, but instead I love them. The brambles must have drawn gallons of blood from me in my lifetime, all in drops oozing from the vicious barb-wounds that heal up and scab in no time, so you hardly think about it.

In fact, I always think about the passage in *Little Big Man* where Jack Crabb describes the initiation of the young Cheyenne braves. Brambles are hooked on to their thighs by the barbs and weighted with logs, so they had to wade about the camp towing the laden bramble-ropes, gritting their teeth as the thorns tore into their flesh and ripped their legs to scar tissue.

People ask how a writer connects with the land. The answer is through work. Look at John Clare, working on the land, knowing it by working on it and being in it for years from earliest childhood. Look at Alice Oswald, working as a gardener for six years, living in Devon and not owning a car, so she walks and bicycles everywhere. Look at Ted Hughes or Henry Williamson, both farming and living with animals.

And when we work on the land, what is our connection with it? Tools, and especially hand tools. Much can be learnt about the land from the seat of a tractor, the older and more exposed the better, but to observe the detail, you must work with hand tools.

Millie. You're a passionate little person – you sit on my table, and when I speak kind words to you, you purr. When I stroke you with kind words, you purr even louder than when I stroke you with my fingertips. And when a train goes by at the end of the fields, or a magpie calls, your ears swivel and focus all on their own, each ear moving independently. So one ear listens to a wood pigeon and another to the slight whirring of the fridge.

Then you yawn, lick your lips, stretch your back, flex your forepaws on my basketwork chair, and purr again to yourself and to me as you settle back on your haunches on the table and begin to wash yourself. You lick your back, you lick your paws, you raise one hind paw and scratch your chin. Then you pause to gaze at Alfie in his black sleekness, stretching out one hind leg like a mutton-chop to wash, to lick.

A family tree is something of a misnomer because it is how we trace our roots, and as the 'tree' bifurcates and proliferates upwards, we go back in time, so that when we reach the leaf tips we are reaching the oldest parts of the tree.

The higher up the tree we go, the deeper we are tracing our roots.

17th July

Last night, a big cloudburst as I lay in the railway wagon, the rain hammering down on the felt roof and resonating through the wooden ceiling, like being inside a drum. It woke me up and then, from 3.30 to 4.30, I lay half asleep, half dreaming. A cloud like a punchball rolled in over the common, suspended low over the land – if I were to punch it, the rain would spill down. It was full to bursting, like the bags of muslin we hang up full of the hot pulp of crab apples or rosehips when we're making jam or wine.

Yesterday, in the rain, a bedraggled little hedgehog appeared in the kitchen, on the brick step. It shuffled round the kitchen, hoovering up bits of food or crumbs. The uneaten cat food was soon polished off and the bowl left gleaming.

Later, I saw its wake of moving grass as it disappeared

through the long grass of the lawn, then swung back across to the vegetable garden, where I think it lives, probably in the lee of the draining board and sink of the summer kitchen, in the sheltered part of the compost heap.

Last night I left out some dried cat food on a log for it, and by morning it had gone.

A spider's web is strong, but only strong enough to catch the size and weight of the prey it wants. It will break under the strain of anything bigger. It is only so strong.

'We'll let the weather clear its throat,' I say. 'We'll wait until it's got this rain and wind out of its system.' 'It must work in some sort of rhythm: just think of the patterns you see on the weather forecast.' I say all this to Rob, about our *Rogue Male* trip to Dorset. 'Rain makes better copy, I know, but bodies glinting in surf under a crystalline Dorset sky make even better words.' Better still when the water's still and clear under Durdle Dor, just rolling pebbles back and forth a half-inch, rocking them on their roundness.

Trees are the measure of things. A tree grows, and we measure ourselves against it. I still have my wooden ruler from school, ink-stained and written on: we used rulers as batons to pass messages covertly round the class. The first measures of length must surely have been cut on sticks. Trees have given proportion to things too. The proportions of this house are decided by the size and length of the timbers available for its construction. The standard width of a timber-framed house or barn, between sixteen and twenty-one feet, is the distance a single beam from an oak will normally span. Of course, you could find longer beams, but they would be correspondingly heavier to move to the building site and lift into position, and so would need greater support. They would also need to be of greater girth to create the span without sagging or flexing in the middle.

Clearing out the workshop in the barn with Alison. Sorting through woodscrews (old-fashioned slot screws, bolts, nails, etc.) and bits of wood kept for woodturning (blocks, etc.). Sorting through my mother's things: drying-up cloths, embroidered tablecloths she never quite finished embroidering, cutlery.

Then, on Wednesday, Alison painting the workshop windows. Out on the common, Michael is cutting the hay on the other side of the railway crossing.

Wood. Two wooden *o*'s at its heart, my grandparents Sidney and Lucy. Two haloes, two theatres, two Globe stages full of stories and love, passion, anger, terrible secrets, warmth, laughter.

That moorhen (another double *o*) was never going to last long. It was my first thought as I watched it standing on one leg like a crane or a stork, stretching its wing and preening, then tucking in its head incautiously to snooze.

People have always got to be over-elaborating things. You can't just go for a swim any more or dive off a board; it has to be flumes and jacuzzis. A walk in the woods isn't enough kicks; you must walk the canopy. You might as well put a ski lift up Kanchenjunga.

The mulberry. The tree that was the basis of all wealth for thousands of years, the Creator of Silk. We kept silkworms at prep school, watched the weaving of their cocoons, and the moth emerging. Yesterday I watched blackbirds, and even a blackcap, eating white mulberry fruit off the tree.

18th–20th July
Trip to Dorset with Rob. We set off from Cambridge at 1.30 p.m. I had been rushing about all morning at Mellis,

packing things in the car that might come in useful. All kinds of food: tins of sardines and mackerel, nuts and raisins, junk chocolate and biscuits, Bourbon creams especially, and baked beans, a solitary tin. Also tools: a slasher, a fearsomely sharp billhook, a triangular bow-saw, an iron griddle for our fire, a corkscrew. Also secateurs and the trusty beech-handled Opinel knife from the Dordogne, where all the farmers and lorry drivers carry them and eat with them in restaurants and *routiers*. Also packed: bivvy bag/pup tent, sleeping bag, matches.

On the way down we stopped at Stockbridge and leant over a railing to admire the brown trout, hanging suspended over gravel in the River Test. Bought muffins and sardines at the delicatessen.

At Mike and Carol's farm, we walked up into the evening meadow on the steep hillside, a mass of flowers: pyramidal orchids, bellflowers, harebells, yarrow, yellow bedstraw, heath bedstraw, dwarf thistles, hay rattle, restharrow, yellow vetch, kidney vetch. And, in the old hedges on edges of the wood, the giant lianas of old man's beard the children swing on and climb.

Dinner of amazing tender lamb, potatoes and broad beans out of the garden. Mike has banned the badgers by pouring buckets of his own pee on their runs. We speak of Vietnam, and a book called *Tunnel Rats* á propos Geoffrey Household and *Rogue Male* and burrowing into the soil – 'going to ground'. Also Thurber's *Thurber Carnival* and a story about a Morgan driver and a driving lesson in 'A Ride with Olympy'.

Next morning we set off for Bridport and Chideock. We drive down the lovely quiet valley, through Winterbourne Strickland with the deserted, steepled parish church near a stream.

Approaching Chideock, we suddenly breast the ridge of the horseshoe of hills Household describes, and all is clear. A deep half-circle of hills with the horns resting on high cliffs by the sea, with Chideock and North Chideock nestling in the centre.

We bought a map (2.5 inches to the mile) from the village stores and drove up to North Chideock, where we left the car in the leafy, shaded car park of the Catholic Chapel of Chideock Manor. It is a hidden, well-wooded, secluded place, reached by walking along a tall box hedge and passing the spreading arms of laurels, limes, planes and oaks. All its traditions relating to the Chideock Martyrs, the Catholic priests, are about hiding, outlaws, covert activities. The Chideock Martyrs actually hid from the authorities and lived in the woods for some weeks – sixteen, I think.

We packed our rucksacks with water and food, and camping gear, and set off up the hill through the village towards Venn Lane, which we entered about midday. Past Venn Farm, going north uphill, it soon became deeply sunken and damp, evidence of a winter-bourne when the land was flooded by the rains. Sticks were jammed into little beaver dams, and the plants of stream banks, brooklime and water mint, grew in profusion, as well as various sedges. Further up the lane we found ourselves walking between 'steep, high banks reaching to fifteen or twenty feet, with the hedgerow trees growing along the bank', as described by Household. To our right was a grazing pasture, rising away up to a rounded down, and to our left the land fell away steeply in other grazing fields, with a double hedge of thick hazel, ash, blackthorn, sallow and holly, with here and there an oak tree or a massive ash.

Towards the high point of the lane, the going became harder than ever, as the brambles, bracken and 'shoulder-high nettles' closed in from either side in a deep, dark tunnel. We persevered, and came to a place beside a huge, slightly ragged ash tree with a trunk some twelve feet in girth. The bank wall of the lane to the east here was fully eighteen to twenty feet, and to the west the hedge was so dense that it would be possible to sit within its cover all day observing the comings and goings in the valley below without ever being seen.

This, we decided, was the most plausible spot for our hero's hideout, burrowed into the sunken lane. However, in terms of strict textual accuracy, we were unable to find solid sandstone here, only ochre sandy earth – could a burrow be safely constructed in such earth? A couple of hundred yards further up the lane, running away downhill to the west, was a dense and ancient coppice of hazel and ash, with a few geans – wild cherries – that had somehow seeded themselves in.

The whole wood, as we entered it, was a dense, dark mass of ochre tumuli, where the badgers had dug the fresh earth from their setts. It was a truly industrial landscape, and the virgin earth had been well trodden into tracks that had all the makings of miniature sunken lanes, given time.

Rob spotted a badger skull on a tump, unmistakable, with its wide, flat jaws and eye sockets, the broad shape of the badger face quite evident in the bones.

A few paces away we came upon the entire skeleton of a badger, possibly poisoned by the local cattle farmers. It was still only three quarters rotted, so must have died quite recently. There was a suspicious low shelter of corrugated iron with some poisonous-looking plastic tubs beneath. It could have been for pheasant feed, but our strong feeling was that this was part of some scheme to poison badgers. Rob's badger skull contained a nest of tiny red ants, which had whitened the bone efficiently.

We walked the full length of the lane as it breasted the ridge and plunged northwards into the Marshwood Vale. We found one or two other promising hiding places, but none as comprehensively deep and inviting and densely vegetated as the one where we had left our rucksacks, camouflaged under bracken fronds in the approved Household style.

We found a dead, fallen oak that could have formed a ladder in and out of the lane, and Rob bravely climbed on to its branches. I took a photograph of him, or thought I did, until we discovered I had failed to press the button hard enough.

We walked the ridge of the entire horseshoe of hills, returning along another lane close to Hell Lane that had more solid walls of sandstone, hollowed into caves here and there by more badgers. On the way downhill, the footpath went through a farmyard, and we were all but attacked by a menacing, yellow-eyed, grey-coated lurcher that made several lunging low runs at us, and almost succeeded in scoring a palpable hit.

Back at the place where we had hidden our rucksacks, we lit a fire in the lane, having dug a little fire pit with our garden trowel and made a hearth and fireback out of some old logs of oak. We were anxious about the smoke giving us away to the farmhouses on the far side of the valley overlooking the lane, so followed the Vlach practice of making a tiny wigwam of sticks, all of small calibre, in order to produce the maximum heat as quickly as possible.

Once it was going well, we kept an eye on the valley downhill to the west, which was unfortunately where the breeze seemed to want to waft our smoke. But the denseness of the hedge and trees above formed such a filter of greenery that the smoke was indistinguishable from the evening mist of the valley by the time it emerged and rolled downhill. Only the cows noticed it, and came up to investigate from the far side of the hedge.

We cooked spaghetti, and were puzzled by the dark brown hue of the water until Rob realized he had left a teabag in the cooking pan. We added chilli con carne to disguise the taste, most successfully.

We lay in the bottom of the lane, reclining on bracken and grass, sipping Glenfiddich and spooning up spaghetti Tuareg-style out of the same cooking pan. Then we made tea, stoking the fire for warmth and light as dusk and then night came on. Pudding was to have been the banana we roasted on the embers, but Rob stepped on it, perhaps because I had earlier made use of it as a demonstration model in a short impromptu lecture on male circumcision in aboriginal initiation cere-monies.

At last we left the dying embers and clambered up the steep bank past the ash tree into the higher field to the west above the lane. Here we camped, well concealed in the lee of the thick cross-hedge that divided the field from the rough pasture that ran uphill to the summit of the down.

We pitched the pup-tents side by side on an almost-level sward and slept soundly in the silence under a mackerel-sky perforated by stars.

Morning broke with a perfect blue sky and tiny fragments of puffy white cloud. The insect hum of farm tractors was starting up far below us in the valley. It was clearly going to be a scorching day. Rob sprang up and strode to the summit of the down, where, he reported, he saw the whole of the Marshwood Vale filled with white mist.

We packed, cleared up our camp of the night before, scat-tering the charred firewood in the bushes and covering our fire pit with turf. Then we set about cutting ourselves the walking sticks we had so sorely missed the day before in our defenceless encounter with the devil-eyed lurcher. Dogs like him are mostly cowards and will melt away on the pretext of having important posts to sniff and mark if threatened.

We chose the coppiced holly directly beside our camp, and

went to work with our penknives on a pair of its straight, greenish poles in a kind of re-enactment of the kind of task Our Hero would have had to perform as silently as possible in his lair. We could have sliced through our holly in seconds with the billhook we had elected to leave in the car: a minor mistake, as it turned out.

It took us half an hour of concentrated clipping and whittling before we had cut down our two holly poles and trimmed them into sticks. But the work seemed well worth while, and the further pleasures of whittling these sticks by the winter fireside will be more than compensation for the sweat of sitting on a prickly bank of holly leaves and sawing away with inadequate tools at an awkward angle.

We hiked out downhill, leaving the whitethroat that had sung to us in our camp and the woodpeckers in the ash tree, washed in the little 'lavabo' thoughtfully provided by the Weld family next to the church, and drove to Burton Bradstock for a bacon sandwich and coffee breakfast outside the Hive Beach Café, overlooking a perfect, deep blue, flat calm sea.

We then swam off the beach under the sandstone cliffs, striking far out in the cool water. We dried off in the sun and made miniature sculptures of the polished pebbles. We swam a second time after a lunch of fish soup, scallops and bacon, then headed for home, mission accomplished.

Household, with his interest in concealment, thinks unconsciously of Chideock and the martyrs hiding in their natural bolt-hole. And the badgers, persecuted and in hiding underground too – a topical touch. Even the mason bees made little burrows there in the wall of the lane.

Roofed by hedge as we were, and diving through tunnels of brambles and thorn, I kept getting hooked like a fish by the scalp. Vertical bramble lianas dangled like fishing lines in our path, and we wove through the lane like two hapless gourmet sardines on our way to be hooked and tinned. Brambles and thorns were impossible to complain about, however, because they were such a vital part of our defences.

We had encountered memento mori at every turn: Catholic martyrs, hung, drawn and quartered at Dorchester Assizes, badger skulls and skeletons, a rabid devil-hound that was probably the reincarnated Major Quive-Smith. Interesting that Chideock is also the site of an extinct castle. We ourselves were searching for an extinct castle of a different kind, one that even had a ballista as a defensive front-line weapon system.

The dappled floor of our retreat.

Buzzards circled and soared above the hills all day, sometimes riding the wind on the ridge almost completely motionless.

Rob has e-mailed me a nice quote from W. H. Murray: 'In short withdrawals from the world there is to be had unfailing refreshment. When his spirit is burdened or lightened, the natural movement of a man's heart is to lift upward, and this is most readily done in the wild, for there it is easy to be still.'

21st July
The kingfisher arrived on Wednesday – or at least I saw it dash along in the deep groove of the common moat behind

the railway wagon, but soundlessly. There have been herons too. I think they come when they sense the water levels dropping, making the fish vulnerable to them.

Is there a correlation between the propensity to take physical risk and a tendency to take intellectual or creative risks? I'm thinking of Samuel Beckett – plunging out of the tops of trees, or riding his AJS motorbike at high speed across the Irish mountains in TT races.

23rd July
A red admiral is resting on the study window frame outside.

Frogs and froglets in the vegetable garden under the endive plants.

The sunlight is rather strong at this south-facing window, so I've made a kind of stained glass of walnut leaves by standing them up in the window; they filter the sunlight into a beautiful, soft green light. This is the real-life William Morris effect – now with *real leaves*!

It is a pigeon-cooing evening, still and dry and quite warm. No sun, but light, high clouds of small cumulus like sweetbreads, or the flecked milk when it goes sour, or even the surface of a brain. There are horseflies about, biting stealthily.

Now there's late sunshine turning the elms golden. I've planted out my sprouting broccoli.

There are butterflies all over the buddleia flowers: red admiral, peacock, tortoiseshell, comma, painted lady, cabbage white, gatekeeper, hedge brown, spotted wood. Nine species.

Houses were once unassuming and unselfconscious. Now they've become suburban, twee, like women made up to the nines, they look only vulgar. When will people learn that less is more when it comes to doing up houses?

These drinker moths: soft, pale bear-brown, furry, chubby, sturdy. The whole insect quivers with life, with the will to live. It's such a thoroughly complex animal, with its antennae, its eyes on stalks, its furriness – why is it furry? Its flurries of activity and drunken movement, then its prostration before my notebook with its antennae lopsided. I want to put them right, but daren't because that would set it racing and burning up energy pointlessly all over again. Should I feed it honey?

Moths are such exquisite creatures. I begin to love them very much. This afternoon I stopped the tractor and grass-toppers and climbed off down just to rescue the most beautiful, big, orange, furry drinker of some kind.

The poor drinker moth on my desk has been poisoned and drugged by a house spider, the giant mother spider that lives on the south window of my study. The innocent moth flew innocently into the web for just an instant last night, and the spider pounced out of nowhere. Her speed was spectacular, as was her technique. She pinned the moth on its back, straddled it with all her many legs and bit it squarely in the breast, seemingly all at the same time. Then, cradling the moth in her undercarriage like a baby in a sling, she moved smartly off, climbing straight up an oak beam and then stopping just as suddenly, puzzled by how to squeeze the moth through the crack of her hideout. I closed the door beside it, and the spider dropped its prey and fled. The moth appeared almost completely dead, its body just pulsating very faintly now and then. It lay immobile on my desk, and I placed it carefully on a pencil box in front of me.

Debby [Moggach] spoke today (at Terence's) of how moths and crickets would enter the little goat house she used to have in the Dordogne in summer and arrange themselves on the wall 'like brooches'. Moths are somehow more cuddly, more like mammals, than butterflies. Perhaps they're more subtle, in their colours and behaviour: the way they walk about, and seem to feel their way with their antennae.

The next night I picked up the drinker moth to take a closer look and it came to life, fluttering and staggering about the desk, but unable to achieve lift-off. The spider venom must have begun to neutralize in the moth's body: somehow its immune system was fighting the poison. It eventually quietened down again on the desk, but in the morning there was no trace of it. It must have flown off into the night.

At night you write out of guilt, but in the morning you write out of hope.

Last night in the railway wagon, a trickle of thunder, a toothpaste squeeze of it along the horizon. Then silence. A few light raindrops on the roof, tentative. Then, after another pause, a downpour kettle-drumming the roof of the old wagon, so loud that it almost drowned the thunder that rolled and tumbled in across the meadows and woods. I lay listening to a symphony. Everything modulated: the rain waxed and waned, there was no wind at all, so it fell straight down, heavily, thudding the wooden roof. And the thunder was stereo thunder, rolling from left to right and back again in the blackness of the horizon. At once a gift from the heavens and an assault on the roof and the land. Lying in bed, dry and sheltered and warm, is a marvellous feeling, sensing the massive increase in humidity, and the subtle wafting of damp breezes, an updraught from the drenched ground.

In the morning, bright sunshine on the flattened grasses.

I have been looking at blackberry bushes for years but never noticed the tiny black beetles that live within their flowers. Each flower may have seven or eight beetles, all busy working the anthers to garner the pollen. Each one is barely more than a millimetre or two long and iridescent black, blue and purple. They look like little jewels in the crown of anthers. And I have no idea what they are called. I might try and find out, but 'blackberry beetles' will do quite well.

Mellis – Robinson's Mill Advertisement. The people at whom the smart, whole-page ad is aimed are 'dog-walkers'. 'Mellis common is ideal for dog-walkers.' Why not just walkers?

Simply 'walking' is conceived as a cranky, long socks and shorts, Ramblers' Association, left-wing sort of thing to do. The affluent have dogs and go 'dog-walking'. 'I'm just going to walk the dog down to the post,' they say, unhooking the Barbour from its peg by the door.

When I draw, I do lots of sketched-in lines that gradually add up to the finished line, which I then draw in with greater firmness once I know for sure where it lies. When I build a house, or turn a bowl on the lathe, I have an outline in mind, but proceed pragmatically, often improvising as I go and adapting the building, or the bowl, to the material. The building may alter if I come across a special window in a skip and decide to make an opening somewhere to put it in. The bowl may alter in form if I come across a fine-looking knot halfway in.

24th July

A long, vivid dream last night: Tony Axon and I were at a school in Walsall, wanting to tell them about our ancestors and their noble traditions as working people. It was the end of term, everyone was assembled, and we were due to go on the stage to address the school: Tony had posters and newspaper cuttings about John Axon the engine driver; I was ready with similar material and stories of the Walsall Anarchists and Joe Deakin. I was wearing a pair of much patched patchwork jeans with floral material in some of the patches – of considerable interest to the girls, who coveted them. The children – adolescents – were dressed like working children of the 1890s or possibly 1920s: smocks and pinafores; and boots for the boys.

The headmaster was Mr Norfolk from Diss Grammar, or someone very like him, and he had a male teacher with him who somehow, during the course of the proceedings, persuaded the head that it would not be such a good idea for us to speak, and we, waiting in the wings backstage, were told that our services would not, after all, be required.

We rebelled, and insisted on speaking, and eventually, having signalled this to the children, managed to get into the hall with them and gather them round us during the temporary absence of the head and his sidekick (probably Mr Matheson = Matheson = maths = all that I most detested and feared at school).

We told the children, with some passion, that they too could educate themselves and stand up for their rights in Walsall, just as our forebears had done. We said they had been noble people, and described life in the goods yard at Wednesbury as a sort of folk university, with books being passed round amongst the workers, and the libraries buzzing. Our message was entirely pro-education and learning, yet we were being treated as deeply subversive.

Last night I bicycled up the common, tracking a barn owl as it slid back and forth above the long grass, the uncut hay, pirouetting and fluttering into a hover now and then and dropping down on to the grass, then rising back up, with something in its talons and adjourning to a tree to consume the prey.

Then two little owls, or even three, in the oak tree outside Wicks's farm, the Hall. One sits on a branch and glares at me, calling its sharp call in complaint.

Quite how the pale barn owl moves at such speed without seeming to flap its wings is a mystery.

26th July

How can I be expected to like squirrels when they have left such a debris of half-chewed walnuts beneath the old tree by the barn? Each year they come and raid the tree and vandalize it like the sort of burglars who have to half smash a house, not content with simply stealing things. I want to say to these squirrels, 'Grow up, act your age. Just take what you need and bugger off.'

27th July

Lying in pain, half feverish with a swollen knee from bashing it on something sharp on the tractor as I jumped on it in a hurry, carting hay this afternoon. It is a still, clear night with a sliver of quarter-moon and a silky mist suspended over the meadow.

I am lying in bed in the railway wagon, thinking of John Wolseley's wagon at Leatherarse Gully.

There is a sort of world train of these wooden railway wagons, and we are all going to the same place: somewhere in the imagination. Transports of delight, we talk of being transported, transported by pain in my case tonight. The wagon embodies every train journey I have ever taken; it embodies my railway roots. I was born to it. It also embodies all the high standards of the old railways as they used to be before privatization. Solid, wooden, oaken, reliable, built to the highest standards, perhaps less than practical, perhaps a little lumbering.

David Holmes – making *bird-boxes*. Paint them yellow! Someone he knew made thirty bird-boxes and his wife painted them colours. Yellow was best – hole more obvious. David's boxes are architectural, amusing, interesting bird-boxes.

29th July

Yesterday I went wandering through the still-standing hay in the home meadow and noticed a beautiful spider's web like a cocoon, binding several tall stalks of cocksfoot together at their flower heads. I bent to look closer and there was an elegant mother-spider, with a clutch of eggs and her long legs stretched out as she carried them to safety, clasped closely to her body. I was concerned that she might disappear when the hay was cut and thought of moving her, then changed my mind because I didn't like disturbing her house.

Then, this morning, Eddie came with his tractor and began cutting the hay. I was busy racing about, on my own grey Ferguson tractor, towing trailers and machinery off the hay meadow to give Eddie a clear run with the cutters. Then, I remembered the spider. It was too late. That part of the meadow had already been cut. I've been worrying about her all day, and shall go out this evening and search in the hay for her. There's not much chance, but it's worth searching. By now, she has probably beaten a dignified retreat anyhow. I haven't even had a moment to look her up in my spider book by Theodore H. Savory, my old zoology teacher from school.

Hardy: *Under the Greenwood Tree* (IV, 'Autumn'). Geoffrey, the gamekeeper, and Enoch, his man, are 'shovelling up ant-hills in the wood' – that is exactly what I did this morning in the Barn Meadow, standing atop the giant anthill in the middle of the meadow and driving in my fork to split it up and level it before the hay-cutters passed over. Queen ants and workers fled in all directions, and there was panic amongst the ants. A field mouse nest inside too.

I walked out across Cowpasture Meadow minutes after the hay was cut, and Eddie and his tractor had left the field to go for lunch. Already there were swallows, a pair of them, swooping low over the rows of cut hay fanned out flat in the intermittent sunshine. They were catching flies, horseflies, I hope. Millie, was out there too, and already on to the scent or movement of a mouse in the hay. Within a minute or two she had pounced and caught a short-tailed field mouse. I went over to see what it was, and she ate it straight away, crunching it efficiently, head first as ever. Later on, she was still roving the same part of the meadow, and I reflected that a single cat couldn't possibly cover more than a fraction of a field at all efficiently, and so dozens of field mice must happily survive by disappearing into their holes at haymaking time. The harvest mice must suffer the most, with their nests suspended in the grasses.

In my cabin I learnt the sheer luxury of daydreaming. It has been my making and my undoing too. How many days, weeks, months, have I lost to it? But perhaps it isn't lost time at all, but the most valuable thing I could have done.

Outside my window I hear industrious tapping, like a gardener at work. Is he banging home a fencing post or mending a gate? It sounds like hammering, but is the vigorous percussion of a thrush's beak and a snail. This thrush is constantly at work at particular anvils round the house: one by the pile of peg tiles next to the ash arch, and one by the woodshed close to a young walnut tree.

1st August

The hedgehog came to my window last night, snuffling, huffing and puffing like Roy Hattersley, and nosed about in the irises for snails. I gave it a handful of dried cat food, which it accepted without even curling up or missing a beat in its wheezing. It reminded me of the sounds lorries and fork-lift trucks now make to indicate that they're reversing. You can imagine in the hedgehog world: 'There goes that Mrs Tiggy-Winkle. I'd know that wheeze anywhere.'

Water provides a metaphor of space for people – of mental space, of freedom, free-floating. All water – river, sea, pond, lake – holds memory and the space to think.

Water levels the spirit too (spirit level). It is the only opportunity we have in the landscape to see a truly level *flatness*; the rest of the landscape, especially in Britain, is always spiky, full of virtual lines – grass, trees, hills, buildings, people themselves, like Lowry's stick-people.

Space in nature, 'wide open spaces', are important for all of us, especially people in cities – we just need to know they're there.

2nd August

It was strange, last night, driving home across Suffolk from the levity of the ukulele orchestra to the just-killed fox on the road at Denham. It was a most beautiful fox, in the pink of condition, its coat thick and a rich, deep red, and, when I gently lifted it up off the road to lay it to rest in dignity be-hind the hedge, it was surprisingly heavy: perhaps twenty pounds, certainly fifteen. There was no blood and there were no marks on it. Its neck must have been broken as it glanced off a car. Strange that foxes, which are supposed to be so clever, can't learn to avoid the headlights of cars. This fox had come out of the Denham woods. It was in such perfect health, yet they say the average life of a fox is no more than three years!

I am not a *twitcher* of woods or trees, forever searching out the tallest, rarest or most exotic trees. I'm interested in individual, and individualist, trees, unusual trees.

I am interested in the society of trees. A wood is a society of trees, and it stands for democracy and society.

Hardly a week goes by without an important story relating to wood and trees; last week, chainsaw commando vigilantes felling sixty plane trees overnight along a French roadside. This week, Mugabe in the Congo – loggers – war.

I walk into my local organic food shop and am invited to sign a petition from the people of Diss in support of the Kayapo Indians in the Brazilian rainforest, whose way of life is threatened by murderous loggers. Why not go to visit them, I think.

A sparrow hawk. Died at 10.00 a.m. outside the kitchen door. Probably kamikaze dive-bombed on to the hosepipe and killed itself on impact. Or was feeding on leftover cat food from the bowl outside the door and surprised by a cat. No blood – warm and supple when I found it. Death caused by a broken neck – neck broken immediately behind the skull.

Weight: 4–5 oz.
Length to tip of tail: 1 ft exactly.
Beak: ½ in. long. Black, shiny, but yellow at base and around nostrils.

Talons: 1½ in. long. Four very sharp, hard, hooked claws, each ½ in. long. Dull yellow, scaly black, needle talons.
Wingspan: 20 in. Wings barred dark brown and pale grey underneath. Five bars of brown. Then speckled brown and white on small downy feathers.
Dark brown on its back, feathers edged in orange/russet, white and brown speckled around head and chin and breast.
Tail 5 in. long. Twelve tail feathers barred brown and pale grey from underneath.
Slender legs 6 in. long. Feathered trousers down to knees.

The favourite Welsh way to dispose of a car is to set fire to it and push it off a hillside so it rolls down in a ball of fire. They now stick in bits of railway line to prevent this at heads of valleys. Kids often steal a 4WD and drive it a long way into a wood and leave it there. Also people drive their cars into woods and leave them, or strip stolen cars of all their useful parts in a wood.

4th August
A flock of tiny goldcrests, the smallest birds we have, tinkling like faery bells in the ash tree. Utterly fearless, feeding on minuscule invisible insects, moving amongst the leaves and bunched ash keys. Often hard to spot, but they come very close to my face, quite without fear. Tiny, weightless birds, bundles of feathers, little pinched beaks. The gang descends,

does the tree over and evaporates as suddenly as it appeared.

Ants, jostling to take off on the nuptial flight scheduled for take off at 5.30 p.m. I'm reminded of Randy Newman's song 'Short People' – the vigorous dissension amongst workers, drones and queens – and today the vigorous dissension between the short-arses of the garden birds, the goldcrests and the wrens.

Drones smaller than ponderous queens, all taking off querulously into apparently aimless flight, all responding to the slightest of stimuli: a change in the weather. The nest under the study step is in perfect sync with the one under the kitchen doorstep forty feet away.

5th August

Why would anyone want to go to live abroad when they can live in several countries at once just by being in England? Yesterday was hot, clammy and humid, with sunshine and dramatic cloud. I might have been in Singapore, fighting for breath. This morning, it is another country, soft and damp after rain, cool and breezy. Last night we were in monsoon India, and, according to the weather forecast, we shall be in the sunny South of France this weekend.

7th August

A damselfly lands on the map I'm reading in the garden. Feminine presence of the resting insect. Intimacy.

9th August

Early sounds: kingfisher, chaffinch, great tit, crow, moorhen, blue tit, goldcrest, mallard, magpie, green woodpecker, wood pigeon. Pigeons mating on the telegraph wires, on my own telephone lines, as I lie reading in the railway wagon. Much noisy flapping and an occasional tumbling off the high wire.

10th August

I am reading Paul Theroux's new book *Dark Star Safari*. An account of a journey from Cairo to Capetown by train, bus, etc., but no planes, all across country the old way. He is passionate about travel as a means of escaping the pell-mell of faxes, e-mail, phones, etc. Just fucking right off out of it, as I would like to do right now.

A hornet flew into my bedroom last night and droned about in the dark, uncomfortably close, so I trapped it in the shade of my anglepoise lamp.

Early evening, I walk down to the railway meadow with spade over my shoulder and rucksack with bin bags in it, dig a few more docks, then pick up sticks of scorched dock stem, lying about like spent arrows on a charred battlefield. I clutch them into quivers and stash them in the black bags, also collecting any seed I find to take away. Little woodlice in the unburnt composting hay and under tussocks on the ground. Hundreds of tiny seedlings sprouting on all the open earth. When I dig up the docks, the earth is very brown and full of worms: it looks festive.

I have been stripping paint off a couple of thirteen-inch pine boards that came out of a skip outside the old Greek Orthodox Church in Camden Town. They were painted brown, in several layers. Gradually, the delicate pale grain of the bare wood begins to appear. The pine is undressed in layers, and reveals itself. It is like restoring a painting.

Idea: use the 'planks' of pallets from the skip at Diss to make a curving bridge or curving outside lawn table, as on the cover of *The Idea of Perfection* by Kate Grenville.

The day when I was seventeen years old a policeman came to the door and told me my father had died that afternoon might actually have been the moment that made me into a conservationist. When I was writing poems like 'Gentian' and later on fighting for Cowpasture Lane, I was wanting back what I had lost. I wanted my father back. I didn't want to lose anything more. I had lost such a big part of my life that I needed to compensate by holding on tightly to everything else.

I wanted not to lose Cowpasture Lane. It was traumatic to lose part of it. I reacted strongly. This may be the source of my passion for conservation. Does this matter? Is it too personal a base? Too emotional a base? Not philosophical enough? Is it even the wrong reason?

14th August

In the late afternoon, having done almost no work at all, I drive down to see Ronnie at Bottengoms. He is in shorts and looking very fit. The stream water is flowing past one end of the house as strongly as ever, and splashing down into a brick culvert with a cool sound that pervades the garden.

Ronnie and I sit either side of the empty fireplace where the Rayburn used to be and talk. He serves up currant cake and tea, then Australian wine (Oxford Landing). We speak of Australia and its unbearable, exhausting heat. Ronnie goes to see D. H. Lawrence's house along the coast from Sydney, a simple place. He says how disgracefully Lawrence was treated by the British. He fled to Australia after the Cornish at Zennor thought he was a German spy. He wrote *Kangaroo* – about

fascism in Australia – and *The Boy in the Bush* – must read!
D. H. L. was on great form with his poems in Australia.

Freud: 'The pattern of our every day lives is repetition' – so
walking through a wood is a constantly reassuring experience,
tree after tree, the same only different, like waves on the sea,
like telegraph poles on a railway journey, or the rhythm of
the wheels on the cracks between the rails.

15th August
Another fine morning and a night in the railway wagon with
Alison after dinner with Gary: a good, simple fish pie of garlic/
ginger/blue onion sweated in oil in the pan, then tipped into
an oblong Pyrex dish of prawns and pollack; sliced courgettes,
lemon and grated cheese added on top and popped into the
oven for a half-hour. Add rice to serve.

The honesty seeds have dried out and need harvesting for
insertion into letters. Also the roses and jasmine are unruly
and need pruning.

I remember the dusty street trees of Moscow, and the lumbering drone of approaching lorries, their outsized wheels designed to accommodate the potholes of Moscow and the even worse craters of country roads. A dense trail of black fumes trails each truck, in one case settling like parachute silk on a flock of starlings on an apple tree. The spiders in my hotel proceed, unhindered by plugs, in and out of the baths and basins. Hooded crows strut hopefully outside a kiosk selling tea from a samovar.

The apple trees along the road to the university, a linear orchard down the central reservation, are dusty and blackened. Melanistic moths no doubt abound. All moths have a tendency to vary their shades of colour, and I was enchanted to look at the subtle gradations in the illustrations in Barry Goater's moth book the other night. The dark spinach has many forms, with shading that ranges from pale green to dark. Hot weather can cause the minor mutations that control these colour changes. Melanism is sometimes the result, as in the black pepper moth during the Industrial Revolution.

Trees make time stand still.

18th August

Today, the kingfisher arrived with his hunting call, which I heard from the vegetable garden, where I was busy in the beginnings of my Kyrgyz outdoor summer kitchen. I had lit the portable cast-iron charcoal-burning stove from Morocco and was cooking a pair of fish and vegetable kebabs. I left them to roast and went over to the pond to see the kingfisher. There he was, springing from his perch on a nettle stem and flying off in a straight line of blue.

The first ash leaves have fallen on to the pond and float above its surface.

21st August

The squirrels raid the walnut tree and I sit indoors munching pistachios. The garden floor under the walnut is a scene of devastation, nutshells and hollowed nuts everywhere. Here and there is a whole walnut, nibbled at the stem and knocked out of the tree but not yet devoured.

The squirrels have begun stealing the cobnuts too. They lie about under the tree, cut down but not consumed so far. The nuts are still green and juicy, so I steal them back.

Tonight I saved a pygmy shrew from Millie. It seemed half-blind, running round in tight circles looking for a way through the grass.

Plenty of wind in the wagon, bashing the ash branches against the stove-pipe chimney, playing it like a percussion instrument. A beautiful sound that I'm quite used to, like the creaking of timbers in a boat, so it actually sends me to sleep. Going out into the dark meadow at night to pee, you could easily mistake the shadows of the young walnuts for deer.

22nd August
The scab came off my keratosis on my arm. Benign it may be, but it's ugly all the same. I shall keep it in a little jar of formalin, white spirit in an inkwell in fact, or clear malt vinegar, pickled. I had stepped out of a hot bath designed to cure my back and knocked off the scab with my vigorous towelling, having forgotten about it.

Today I feel at last there's the possibility of a clear run: writing in the morning; lawn mowing or hedge cutting or apple planting in the afternoon.

I live in the Waveney Valley in Suffolk, and the names of the villages here evoke the wooded place this once was: Fressingfield, Metfield and Cratfield were clearings, felled out of the surrounding woods, fragments of which remain. Palgrave was a grove of poles, in other words a coppice wood for roofing poles, long and straight. Redgrave was a grove of reeds for thatching them. Thornham, Oakley.

What were once lapwings on the plough in late autumn or winter are now seagulls on the gleaming new sods in August. A footpath sign points forlornly at uninterrupted stubble as though pointing at something departed.

This morning I am reading Oliver Rackham on ponds and moats, p. 365 of *History of the Countryside*, and a dragonfly comes and perches on the page. It flicks its head now and again, like a nervous twitch, then flies off for a moment, only to return. Its wings cast beautiful latticework shadows, magnified by the angle of the morning sun, across the page. When it eventually flies away five minutes later, there is justice in that it alights on pale grey concrete. It must enjoy every last scrap of reflected light.

Digging docks in the railway field in eighty degrees of dead-still heat is, astonishingly, extremely satisfying – mopping a wet brow, thinking how hard work is the best, and perhaps the only way to come close to the heart of the land. The land opens its heart to you, and admits you to a greater level of intimacy.

Only by digging the docks could I learn how their roots go, how strong their tree-like tap roots are, or how the tap root often divides into two, so that when you uproot and overturn the dock, it waves the pair of them in the air like the legs of a defrocked milkmaid tumbling in a haystack.

Digging up docks one by one, instead of simply driving a tractor and sprayer through them in a matter of minutes, is highly satisfying not because of any holier-than-thou, smug feeling of organic sanctity, but because it is just a far more interesting and harmonious thing to do.

In the course of it I notice the half-burnt stems of the docks lying about the meadow; striped deep crimson and black, they have the same jungle look as the stems of horsetail, bamboo or Japanese knotweed. But they also have the look of red-hot iron, as though the fire has somehow tempered and toughened them.

As soon as you see a plant in its entirety, below the plimsoll line as well as above, you want to know what is in its roots – what properties they hold stored up, medicinal, perhaps, or culinary; or what lives in its roots – what larvae feed parasitically on them, as the witchetty grub does on the roots of tumbleweed.

23rd August

There must be a Moroccan word for the little cast-iron stove I'm cooking on in the summer kitchen. It is incredibly efficient, and I realize how much we have to learn about energy conservation and fuel economy from people in places where fuel is scarce. Out in the Moroccan desert, wood fuel is at a premium, so you want to keep your cooking fire small, compact and efficient.

The earthenware tagine pot is exactly the right size to fit snugly into the cast-iron fire-bowl, which holds a tiny fire of kindling sticks and a half-dozen pieces of charcoal. The other night I put on a dozen charcoal pieces, and they were more than enough to cook a lamb tagine. Last night I cooked beetroot on it too.

Tonight, at nightfall, the owl comes by and screeches twice outside my study. I get out the sound kit hastily but too late. Silence. He is gone.

The kingfisher has been on the moat too.

Eventually I set off for Devon and drive as far as the service station twenty miles short of Bristol. Leave Mellis at 5 p.m., arrive there at 8.30 p.m., then break down at the petrol pump – burst my hydraulic pipe on power-steering system behind steering rack. RAC man comes, fluid all over the tarmac, police car comes swanning up with lights flashing: 'Switch off that mobile immediately – you could blow up the entire petrol station.' Good thing too, I think. At 11.30 p.m. RAC recovery lorry arrives and loads up the car, and I decide that instead of going back to Norfolk, turning tail, I should head on down to

Newton Abbot and the Audi garage there. A long, tedious, two-hour drive to Newton Abbot – the driver insists on closing all the windows, smoking and eating crisps all the way – where I meet Alison. We leave the Audi in the garage entrance. No letterbox at the garage so leave the keys next door and a note on the windscreen. Instant feeling of loss of independence and freedom. Claustrophobic. I pack tent and sleeping bag in rucksack, ready to camp at the service station if necessary.

Alison and I walk up and over Hameldown and down to the Miner's Pool; we find an old mine-working pit, with a great mossy sallow and some rowans growing out of it. A tangle of twisted branches grope out of the dimness for light. The disused mine was at West Combe – the combe was full of oaks, rowans, sallows, all mossy and bent.

We disturb a solitary woman sitting reading a book beside the Miner's Pool. She rises, grey, elegant plaits and handsome lovely face, and spotted black and white dog, friendly. Probably lives in the house along the track of concrete.

We walk back uphill through a huge storm – sleety rain, freezing on the soaked trouser legs. Boots, no socks, squelching – full of water.

Dartmoor – a treeless landscape that was once forested, then clear-felled by the iron and tin smelters.

Now only a few solitary hawthorns or rowans.

24th August

Dartmoor. A great walk with Alison from Batworthy Farm, across the moor towards the stone rows of Shovel Down (two parallel rows of stones running north–south, which must have been a processional route for rituals or celebrations close to Scorhill stone circle). We then turn due west and walk across open moor to the bend in the Teign and the swimming hole known variously as 'Teign Turn', 'Turn Teign' and 'The Elephant's Tail'. Lovely, deep (six-foot) pool some twenty or thirty feet long and wide, with level picnicking grassy banks either side. Three friends and a little girl are picnicking, and the mother and child paddle into the shallows near where the pool has been dammed, by the local swimmers I suppose. We follow the banks of the river – emperor dragonflies, dark shadows of trout dashing into the cover of the bank, water buttercups. There are small, elongated islands now and again, stiff with heather and miniature gorse, and wherever the river gushes through a jumble of rocks, there are twisted, crouching sallows and ferns and mosses. I photograph a bent and windswept flat-top hawthorn beside the river. Solitary, as so often. Yesterday saw a single hawthorn with a raven perched in it.

Higher upriver we find sandy banks, like miniature cliffs in the peat, where dozens of wasps – Sand-wasps? Dark bodied but perceptibly striped – buzzed about as though locked out of home or waiting to be let in. Why? I must look them up. Same phenomenon, around 5 p.m., on every sandy bank, both sides of the river. I see two or three lizards. There is a miniature harebell or campanula near the river, and ripe whortleberries. A treeless landscape, this part of the moor. We reach a fence and wall, a boundary, and another time it will be good to walk on upriver to the deserted Teign Head Farm and eventually to the Teign head itself.

In the evening, I walk up to Moretonhampstead Church and find a big wych-elm growing out of a stone wall and hedge bank in one corner of the churchyard (northern corner).

At Yeo Farm, just past the river bridge downhill of the farm as you descend from Batworthy to Chagford, there's a lovely wood pasture of small oaks and a hazel copse in a dell to the right of the road, near what was once a little 'dame school' where wealthier Dartmoor farmers' sons and daughters used to go.

Everywhere I go, in Devon, or in Somerset, the men are out in the churchyards mowing every blade of grass in sight. Nobody seems to care that Francesca Greenoak has written her book about churchyards, or that they can be such rich repositories of parish plants that may be rare or locally extinct, or that creatures like grass snakes, frogs, toads, lizards, slow-worms, hedgehogs, field mice and voles of all kinds depend on long grass for the cover they need to survive.

Here I am with a cricked neck and a stiff back from too much Green Man hunting. I've been lying on my back along oak pews, or twisting my face upwards to try to make out the details of the features of the Green Men in the roof bosses of South Tawton or Sampford Courtenay churches in Devon, or craning up to look at bare-breasted painted angels in Muchelney Church in Somerset. I couldn't help but see the bosoms and their ripeness and rosiness reflected in the apple trees in the orchards outside, in the churchyard and church house, and in the farm orchard by the barn of the abbey opposite.

Why don't vicars plant orchards in their churchyards? Especially in Somerset, where there are orchards leaning their branches in over the churchyard walls all around. The apple is such a symbol of continuing life, of eternity, of completeness and goodness. Surely it is the perfect churchyard tree? And its fruit could be harvested for the harvest festival and then distributed amongst the parishioners.

You approach my place along a bumpy track across a Suffolk grazing common. It is hidden behind tall trees beyond a moat that runs around parts of the perimeter of the common – a strip of spinney, ash, maple, goat willow, holly and old, gnarled thorn trees. You can just see the chimney above the trees. I thought when I first saw it that it must be a fantasy, a form of East Anglian mirage, and I still do. Its grip on reality, its relation to the rest of the world, remains tenuous at best. Crossing the moat on my return here, and making my way past the ash and the walnut – a pair of guardian trees that watch over the place, throwing shade, algae and mosses on to the roof, and regularly damming the rainwater gutters with composting leaves – I always experience the relief a badger must feel as it eases itself back into the sett after a hard night's foraging.

A warm, sunny day, but cooler in the evening, and a change to wind and rain said to be on the way. Emperor dragonflies about, and the carp very frisky and bold in their planet orbits of the pond.

I must have trees about me. The more I become involved with the lives of the animals and plants of this place, the more passionately I find I dislike what is being done to them in other parts of my village. It becomes personal. If the man next door shoots the cock pheasant who struts on my lawn every morning and takes raisins almost from my hand, how should I feel towards him? Has he not murdered my friend?

All through the spring and early summer breeding season, I deliberately leave as much long grass as I can for small creatures – insects, spiders and snails as well as mammals and amphibians – to breed and make their homes.

By the fluctuating volume of the trains going past the bottom meadow, I can forecast the weather. If they're loud, it is going to rain. The droplets of water that constitute increased humidity carry the sound waves better than the dry air that brings sunny weather. If the intervening meadows were a swimming pool, the trains would be deafening.

Iain Sinclair has been writing about King's Cross and St Pancras, and Aidan Dun. He returns yet again to Dun's 1955 poem 'Vale Royal' about Blake's vision of St Pancras as a sacred place, a centre of energy, with St Pancras, the boy martyr, presiding over it, with Mary Wollstonecraft buried there, and Thomas Hardy's ash tree rising, growing out of a rubble of gravestones like a stack of books in a bookshop. A tree rising out of the dead – Yggdrasil, the world tree, a great symbol of life in the face of the developers who have been under criticism for expunging this place ever since Dickens wrote his great passage on the coming of the railway to Camden in *Dombey and Son*.

29th August

I admire the great skill of my dentist Brian Williams. His conservation of my teeth is somehow like my work on the hedge, endlessly working back and forth along the rows of teeth, as I work back and forth along the hedge.

The great majority of the conservation work in this county goes on inside people's mouths. We should appreciate our dentists for the craftsmen and women they are.

Inside your own mouth, a crumbling molar is an oak tree falling to its knees. Half grooming ape, half tree surgeon, your dentist sends men inside your mouth with tools to shore up the tottering gnashers. We mourn a lost tooth as we mourn the loss of a loved tree, or rejoice at its saving, springing from the dentist's chair rejuvenated. I know of nothing so debilitating as toothache. (Dentists are kindred spirits with anyone with an interest in conservation.)

Digging over at an outlying corner of the vegetable garden this afternoon, I unearthed a length of chain with a rusted spring clip on one end and recognized it as a goat tether I had last used twenty years ago or more. It was about a foot down under a retired compost heap and must have been buried, at least in part, by the ploughing of earthworms.

To discover my own life becoming archaeology like this was a shock. I had now lived my way into a timespan in which my own artefacts, tools or relics had become archaeological finds.

I was no longer digging up things from my own past metaphorically but literally.

This morning I noticed the roof over my library was sagging in one corner, so I went up a ladder and fixed it. The tile battens had rotted and collapsed, and the felt was in poor shape, so I replaced both, then replaced the tiles. A good feeling.

I also spotted the hornets' nest. For weeks now, I have been under siege in my study at night from hornets. They drone in across the garden like Brabazon bombers, and I shut the window and door before they can get in. If they succeed in flying inside, I have a yoghurt pot and a postcard ready to trap them as they lumber towards the light; I then release them outside.

No writer should bear ill will towards hornets: they are the inventors of wood pulp and paper, the original paper-makers.

At night, they bash themselves against my study window, flying straight towards me at my desk out of the dark. A dozen of them crawl about on the other side of the windowpane, allowing me to measure them up with a ruler. Each one is exactly an inch long, and tubby, like a weekend footballer in a striped vest.

Every writer likes a story with a sting in its tail. This is the real thing, on a grand scale.

The first time I ever encountered a hornet here, I was up a ladder at the top of a chimney. I came down that ladder scarcely touching a rung and sprinted away across the lawn. When I looked back, the hornet was still hovering harmlessly about the chimney. I have since learnt that they are peaceable, harmless enough creatures as long as you don't actually attack their nest. I have often encountered them, usually in the kitchen at night, and have never been stung. Last year they nested above the water tank. This year they have settled inside the roof of a dormer window upstairs. They are no bother at all, and I see no reason to exterminate them.

Yesterday I took the tractor and toppers down to the Railway Meadow and topped the western side of it, decapitating docks and thistles. It is very tussocky, and will need some chain harrows dragged over it too, in the autumn (fast approaching). Today I shall light the vegetable garden bonfire.

Sunny and clear and warm in the middle of the day; cooler, even a chill in the air, on my evening bike ride 7.45–8.15. The fields are already being ploughed. I passed several completely ploughed, with the heavy clay sods baking hard in the sun. Surely this means a huge loss of water and moisture from the land at a crucially dry time of year? What effect will the drying out of the stubble field and its wildlife have on the woodland?

Sleeping north–south does seem to improve the quality of my slumbers. Last night I did 12.20 to 7.30 a.m. straight through, with plenty of dreams: a rope securing a log floating out to sea somewhere in Greece or Spain in a fishing port. I am going through the town seeking the rope, having come down from a high mountain.

Sleeping, lying north–south, here in the railway wagon – away from the house, separated by half a field, tucked into a hedge, the wagon's back to a moat to the north, and its open door facing south and plenty of air – does make a big difference.

All this raises the question of geomancy. I felt more and more certain, as I built my house, that the geomancer must have been a most important figure in early settlements. How did people decide on this place rather than on that or on the other to site their house? I am more and more convinced of the truth of camping – because we are all in transit through life – and of deserts, a kind of tabula rasa to an artist, full of potential and actually full of life.

How did the geomancer decide on this place? Or have

I put the question right? How was this place decided for the geomancer? How was its exact location revealed to him? We shy away from such questions now, but in the late 1960s and early 1970s, the time when I settled here, such ideas, such questions, were very much alive. Plenty of people I knew then would think nothing of dowsing over a map, let alone a place, to discover the numinous hot-spots.

We all experience a geomancy when we come to decide on a camp site, and, most particularly, the precise spot and orientation for the pitching of the tent. It must be absolutely level, or as near as you can find, and there must be some degree of shelter. On the other hand, it must not be under a cliff down which loose rocks may tumble in the night, or in the dry bed of a winter-bourne that could suddenly flood in a storm. But these are mere practical considerations. There is yet another thing that makes a place feel right. And nobody knows what that is. Some places simply seem to be blessed. Others are unquestionably cursed. I know a dark, deep pool in what was once a quarry in the Malvern Hills where I instantly felt a doom and deep foreboding, and would not swim, or even linger there by its banks.

When I first settled here two questions interested me. First, what made me choose this place above all the others I had found in Suffolk, Norfolk, Herefordshire and Wales? I had even considered a derelict watermill deep in a Cornish valley, and a railway station at Dulverton Junction in Devon, and a crossing keeper's cottage near Denver in the fens.

There had been Denver Hall itself, and Snore Hall just up the road, near the banks of the Black Drain, one of the main channels out of the fens on to the Ouse. But this was the place that spoke to me, the place I fell in love with.

The second question was how did the very first people who settled here decide this was the place? At some point, perhaps long before the building of this particular house about 1550, this was all wild lane, and people came along and chose it as their home.

The presence of springs must have been a vital factor, and the presence of the common for grazing. Siting the house at the moated perimeter of the common, like most others in the village, suggests the early settlers were graziers.

What a pleasure and a change to see a real live bull with cock and balls, full scrotum of his own sperm, grazing harmoniously with his harem on the common.

The farmer, however tamed and highly pedigreed his cows, still carries the magical connection with our Neolithic ancestry most of us have lost. People grope at it with dogs and cats, even guinea pigs and goldfish, budgerigars or a tortoise on the lawn. But it isn't quite the same as the cow and, even more, the bull. The horse is another question altogether: mostly, apart from gypsy piebalds, tamed, subjugated and above all gelded out of all potency. Slaves used to hard labour every day. They are now running to fat and silliness in the vacancy of their indolence.

30th August

Tomorrow, I shall make steps up to the railway wagon entrance out of willow logs, using sections of trunk from the tree I planted at one end of the moat. I dug it up in Cowpasture Lane and carried it in across the field.

Tonight I write by candlelight and a torch in the railway wagon, where all I hear is the ticking of the clock.

A spider has attached one corner of its web to the lid of my lap-top, so that when I opened it to do a type-up of my morning's longhand riff, I inadvertently upset the spider's entire universe, and it went into spasm in the almost invisible trampoline of its devastated web.

It has slung its web smack in front of a framed close-up photograph of orchids and a mass of other spring flowers in the wild profusion of the Coliseum in Rome. I wonder if it thinks it is in a meadow? Or in Rome, even?

31st August

Commas are flying on plums and fruit. Already the sallows on the track are up to six feet after their coppicing in March to April. The hazel in the wood is up three feet and the ash too is back in business at the front spinney. The ash-arch tunnel is up three or four feet and producing ash keys.

Ramparts of ripe black blackberries surround the old green lorry I used to drive to school on Wednesdays, so the Sixth Form could all pile in and we could drive out to an old wych-elm at Wortham and sit under it and read *Howards End* beside the *Datura stramonium* – the hallucinogenic thorn apple.

The plums are ripe and deep purple and maroon on the tree, hiding behind leaves like the elusive courgettes in the vegetable garden.

A night of black imaginings and dark dreams that jolted me awake in the pitch darkness with only a curled-up cat between me and the abyss. Her gentle purring brings me round, and I think of all the eras of the house delineated by the cats who reigned here. Like the Elizabethan or Caroline or Georgian ages, this house has the first age of Willy and Woody, the grey and the tortoiseshell. Then Alice, then Choirboy and Gringe, successive ginger toms, then Twinkletoes, mother to generations of fine kittens, fathered by a feral tom cat with flowing white fur. Then Millie and Alf, or Millicent and Alphonse to give them their proper names. Alphonse is a son of the white feral tom and half wild himself, born in a hedge and only very gradually tamed, still only half tame.

The cats are all buried beneath the ash arch, which is sited on the old midden of the house, still wildly fertile and full of phosphates from the original feeding and bones of the people who lived here; huge eight-foot nettles and hogweed and hops grow up there every year.

September

1st September

A speckled wood butterfly on the windowpane to the north of the study. Always on the north windows. Always speckled wood. Three spots on the lower wing, one spot on the higher. It sits on the windowpane trembling, like living stained glass. Pale beige windows in its brown wings. The serrated outline of a leaf on its wing edges/borders. Target-shaped spots. The dark brown penumbra shows up the spots.

2nd September

Why do commas sit on my hazel bender in the afternoon sun, while tortoiseshells sit on the brick terrace and speckled woods drink deep at the wounded plums on the plum tree?

Pine is a wood I like much better in its material form as timber than in its vegetable life as a tree. Pine is the stuff of Shaker furniture and of cottage kitchen tables.

I once made half my living from pine during the very early days of stripped pine. I was stripping pine in my mother's backyard in Headstone Lane in the early sixties, driving out to remote junk-men in places that seemed the end of the world, like Molehill Green in Essex, somewhere the far side of Bishop's Stortford, or buying from Mr Carr near Audley End – he had an emporium of chaises longues, Windsor chairs, smoker's bows, corner cupboards, chests of drawers with white porcelain handles, Welsh dressers, blanket chests.

The junk-men never looked happy. They were hunched and wrapped up in pullovers and overcoats, or jackets with leather patches on their elbows. The pained expressions they wore were professional, always looking unhappy about the prices they were offered by hopeful bargainers, or about the escalating prices at the auctions, never satisfied.

I love the graininess of pine, the way the wood erodes into little valleys between the lines of the grain, and the knots that appear like dark brown islands on a sea chart, with the wavy lines of the grain like currents or contours.

Pine left bare and simply oiled with linseed or walnut takes on the patina of its daily use. It absorbs the grime and sebaceous oil of the hands and elbows that rest on it deep in thought. It glows and grows golden in the sunshine that slants in through the window.

Wood is by no means just brown, and yet it so often is brown. I have always liked the colour brown. I like brown corduroys. I like the varied subtle browns of a tweed overcoat. I like brown leather shoes. I liked the brown and cream of the old Pullman railway carriages.

I began to ask my friends, 'What colour is wood?' 'Depends which kind,' they said.

Holly is very pale, almost white. Ash is blond and sometimes nearly silvery inside, flashing like silk as you move it about under the light. Yew is definitely red, orange and yellow. But elm is distinctively brown, and seasons down into a lovely nut-brown. Oak may be white or brown, depending on the activities of the beefsteak fungus in its roots. All trees have fungi living symbiotically in their roots, an arrangement of mutual benefit to both plants. One of the incidental benefits of beefsteak fungus is that it bestows a lovely depth of brown on the timber in an oak. And as oak ages, the tannins in the wood cause it to darken and become the rich brown that surrounds me here in this house.

Instrument-makers often choose wood for its colour as well as for its timbre. Rosewood for violins, and the pale gold of straight-grained, slow-grow King Billy pine for a violin.

4th September

I spent the afternoon lying under the choir stalls of Norwich Cathedral looking at misericords carved out of six-inch-thick blocks of solid oak. Some of the hinged seats have lovely knots in them. Jayne and I ducked under the ropes and were busy lifting seats and examining their undersides under the disapproving glare of a deaconess who came in and switched on the lights. 'We're looking for the Green Man,' said Jayne. 'He's over here,' said the deaconess. 'And you won't have to climb under any more ropes to see him either.'

There were choirboys' sweet papers under the cushions.

Cricked neck again, peering up at roof bosses in the nave. Great one of Adam and Eve and the apple tree, and of Noah's Ark; rows of little medieval faces peering out of post holes, then a row of sheep and cows.

Elbow-rest carvings of faces, angels, etc., nearly worn bare by generations of fidgeting choirboys.

What is so strange this year is how few insects are eating the plums. A huge crop, ripe for the eating, yet where are the wasps? Or even flies? And few swallows either. I strongly suspect this is connected with the spraying of a field of tick beans next door to Cowpasture Lane.

As soon as you have farm or garden machinery, you have straight lines. It is just too inconvenient to mow round curves and circular boundaries. A tractor towing a grass-cutter much prefers a straight line, and that is why our farming landscape is the way it is. Even a ploughing team of horses prefers a straight line, as in the old ridge-and-furrow patterns. A circular wooden stockade around the garden is a tempting idea, but would be difficult to mow around from the field side for the tractor. I would scythe it instead.

5th September

Another lovely, fine, dry morning – hardly a drop of rain for days – earth very dry. Grass seeded in vegetable garden. Spiders' webs everywhere in the garden today, garden spiders with a white cross. Two crane-flies struggling in a web at the corner of my door frame in the study. Ungainly legs flailing the air.

6th September

Yesterday I noticed that on the tin roof of the woodshed, where I have lined plums in rows in the valleys of the corrugated-iron roof to dry in the sun as prunes – an experiment – a spider has noticed the numbers of visiting fruit flies and other insects, and constructed a funnel-necked web immediately next to the rows of plums. It has got lucky straight away and a dozen victims were struggling in their silky bonds by the late morning.

7th September

Spiders invented abseiling, paying out their own silky thread, lowering themselves at will, letting the silk thread run or check as they please.

Dolomedes/Archimedes. The fen raft spider, *Dolomedes*, like his near namesake, understands the principles of physics and the ways of water. He knows that the sum total of the surface tension acting on his eight legs on the water will keep him afloat. He is also ancient and wise, and lives by his powers of observation.

10th September

'All too short a span' is the phrase that keeps coming to me as I think of moths. None of them lives long, and nature has not even bothered to equip many of them with the means of feeding: 'mouth parts', as they are elegantly termed in lepidoptery. There is a kind of Zen of moth-mounting, as there is of flower arranging, which dictates that moths be displayed with wings outspread, as if they were butterflies out basking in the midday sun on a sunny day. It is entirely artificial, and it makes it hard to identify moths in real life, because in real life moths settle with their wings folded. They only spread them out in flight, when they are a whirring blur.

It is natural to associate moths with death because they generally fly by night. Some of them, like the death's head hawkmoth, are overtly macabre. They themselves are liable to meet an untimely end, in the bellies of bats or birds or spiders, and their main defence is camouflage. This leads to their great beauty: the range and subtlety of their colours and designs.

'Stridulation' is the washboard effect of a grasshopper rubbing its back legs against its serrated thorax. Crickets sing this way, so do the larvae of the stag beetle and death-watch beetles, which head-butt the wooden beam they are tunnelling through to make the characteristic clicking. They are percussionists; they bash their heads against the wood.

17th September
To Orford Ness with Rob. He arrives in a tin fart-box on hire, and we load up a pair of holly walking sticks. Cook bacon and eggs and strong coffee to revive Rob after a cold night out on a bed of shingle and sand on Blakeney Point. He had woken with very stiff muscles down the left side of his back, and I apply ointment to heat and relax them, then we do stretching exercises against the kitchen door.

We drive down the ley line of flint churches across Suffolk to the coast: Eye, Horham, Stradbroke, Laxfield, Ubbeston, Sibton, Yoxford, Snape, Iken (nearly), Orford.

At Orford we register our names at the National Trust Office and are told we must stick to the marked paths and roadways on the Ness. We take the ferry across, and are met by a nice warden who tells us all the same things all over again. 'There's unexploded ordnance all over the place out there.' Actually, they don't want us disturbing the plants or the shingle. If there were any unexploded bombs here, we would never be allowed on the Ness at all.

Rob and I talk a lot about Sebald on the way over, and about eco-feminism. Sebald on Orford Ness is very gloomy.

He sees a hare and notes its terrified eyes. He feels the oppressive weight of the military might that was being tested in the bomb ranges here. When did he come over here, we wonder. How did he arrange it?

We stick to the paths and walk out towards the distant horizon of red and white striped lighthouse, and a few concrete buildings. We head first for the Bomb Ballistic Building, black-painted brick and concrete, but we climb some ringing steel steps and arrive in a first-floor room that almost feels cosy by comparison with all the echoing concrete. It is panelled with six-inch pine boards tongued and grooved and stripped back trendily to the naked grain. Oblong windows give graphic panoramas of the lighthouse on the beach. It's hard to see, in the grey light, where the shingle desert ends and the sea begins. Except it isn't a desert but full of sea plants.

All the plants are like barbed wire: thistles and teasels and brambles and prickly leaved compositae. Rabbits shit on old beams of oak from an extinct boat. Hen harriers hover and drop delicately now and again into the grass and bounce up again.

Notices in old pre-fab concrete buildings with asbestos roofs. Richard Deacon-like scrap metal lies about the shingle waves.

Sounds. A soundscape of wind, ringing steel of the bridge over Stony Creek as we stride across, our holly sticks running along the chainlink fence and vibrating, or tap-tapping on the steel floor. Feet on the ringing steel stairs or crunching through shingle on the windswept beach. Wind hooting across the neck of a water bottle, the note deepening as I drink the water level down.

Lichens on the concrete like maps of all the Pacific Islands where they tested nuclear bombs. Dozens of different lichens on the concrete.

Buildings left as ruins. Even quite ugly buildings begin to look beautiful as ruins.

On the beach we crunch along, wishing we had brought a tape recorder to record the soundscape of the place. The clack of holly sticks against the pebbles. Rob searching for special hag stones and flecked flints; me picking up bits of wood with the grain raised – by erosion of the softer sapwood between the lines of tough grain – and burrowed by shipworms.

In a glass display cabinet in a building called 'Power House', a selection of pebbles and driftwood from the beach. People have left a few things on top of the glass. I hope they leave them there. A turned wooden screw-stopper of a lemonade or beer bottle. Amazing piece of work, with the pinholes where it fitted into the lathe still showing clearly. The barbed-wire flora of thistle, the small-leaved, stringless nettle *Urtica minor*. An ancient piece of yew-wood flotsam.

When we at last reach the sea, forbidding and turbid grey-brown, there is a makeshift wooden bench, and someone had collected bricks and bits of concrete and built a little stove-like structure right at the edge of the shingle ridge. No fire had been lit in it; it was just a little sculptural den, a tiny cave, a fragment of shelter on seven miles of the most exposed beach in Britain.

A patch of brilliant crimson samphire to the left of the road as we walk out, raked by the invisible beam of a hovering hen harrier's eye.

Square concrete blocks the size of small chests of drawers, each with a steel ring in the top, for marching protesters or spies, a surreal touch that suggests they are portable. Dumb-bells for fork-lift aerobics. Machines need regular exercise, same as the rest of us. Try shutting away a car for a year or so, and then try starting it up.

We find ourselves walking across steel duckboards, perforated with circular holes four inches across. Some sort of humus has collected in these circles, dirt from people's boots, rabbit dung, windblown sand, and each one supports a different group of tiny plants. It would be interesting to study them more closely.

How many people visit Orford Ness each year? Three thousand. Many are National Trust members, and in summer holidays there may be a hundred a day. Today there are four of us, or seem to be. The warden has a bicycle and goes off to the Police Tower to sit and keep watch. There's a long history of espionage here.

All the wild, remote places in Britain are commandeered by the military, yet by an odd irony their wildlife often thrives and survives as nowhere else as a result of two main factors. First, the places aren't farmed or subjected to the ravages of agriculture. Second, they are often fenced off and people are excluded from them, apart from the odd soldier, the military police or tank.

Many of our wildest, most beautiful places are under occupation, and we are denied access. Orford Ness still belongs to the military because, so we are told, it is a minefield. As Englishmen, we cannot freely walk our own country because it is mined, and we are under threat of death.

Salisbury Plain, Tyneham and Worbarrow Bay in Dorset, the Breckland surrounding Watton in Norfolk, St Kilda, Dartmoor – all are dominated by the war machine. They are no longer places of peace: they are firing ranges, and there are unexploded shells underfoot. So they are 'no man's land'. On top of the threat of being blown up, there's the nuclear question. Why are the pagodas of Orford Ness out of bounds? This makes me feel like a schoolboy and want to break bounds.

19th September

I found a dead female stag beetle in the flower urn, drowned by me with a watering can, I think, and a rare species now too.

Jayne is here, drawing the spinney on the common in its own charcoal, catching the light slung across autumn ponds or flooded across the common through its tree fringe. She says she is constantly *chasing the light*, that this is an obsession of landscape painting and its great bane. As a landscape painter, you are always racing to get things down, to show a tree and the shadow it casts across a pond before that shadow has moved round on to its bank.

By drawing the spinney in its own charcoal, she's expressing its essence *in* its essence. She works on the ground, spreading out a big board of cardboard and unrolling a scroll of printer's paper, cadged from a printer in Norwich. Halfway through one of the pictures she discovers the printer's boot print where he walked over it. Her idea is to make an endless scroll, a frieze, a Bayeux Tapestry, of the woodland fringes of Mellis Common.

In the morning the trees are backlit, and in the evening the westering sun highlights their leaf colours, with the textures of the undulating hedge and woodland like a seashore, or the shores of a great lake. It takes Jayne two days to get the hang of these woods, and how on earth to portray them. She wants to avoid what have become the clichés of local art: a kind of trendiness characterized by a cartoon approach, a graphic rendering of detail, usually with handwritten notes across the page, jottings identifying field names or tree species, or the presence of garden warblers or shield beetles.

The Sticks. This is supposed to mean the countryside, the places people go away to at weekends from 'the Smoke', or disappear to in order to raise a young family and grow vegetables – they are never heard of again.

22nd September
I'm picking up the apples. *Je ramasse les pommes*. The windfalls at Mellis – hard, back-bending work. There was a big wind and storm yesterday, so now lots of Bramleys all over the lawn.

Certain things are missing from Mellis Common this year, not entirely explicable through natural phenomena – neither weather nor temporary changes in climate. There are no skylarks singing. Very few butterflies. No buttercups on the fifty-acre section of the common known as Compartment 2 at the west end. No wild flowers on areas that are suspiciously rectilinear – no buttercups – next to no cuckoo flowers.

The simple pleasures of old-fashioned bird-watching are good enough for me. I still prefer the modest excitement of a woodpecker arriving on my apple tree, a flock of goldfinches in winter, or even a moorhen strolling across the lawn. This is about advanced bird-watching.

Trees are defenceless organisms in relation to man. Their only defences are longevity and fecundity.

Therefore they are places of sanctuary, of refuge for the persecuted or the hunted.

Return to the woods is like our nightly return to the unconscious.

Staverton Thicks. Oak, holly, beech, leaf mould and ferns on forest floor. Pine beyond. An old gate into a ride and dells. Scythe-shaped stools.

A pigeon feather and a magpie feather stuck in the trunk of an old oak. Also a charm hung on a branch – a necklace of green cut glass – this is witchery. An oak and holly growing out of the same root.

Full of growing things. Ancient rowan, gnarled, bowed, holed, twisted. An ancient chestnut, huge and twisted, and a holm oak too. Some hollows run right through the tree, so you could pass a child right through, like the eye of a needle. And cobwebs all up the tree in the twigs.

The bracken becomes impenetrable in the middle; you can be tripped or stopped by the branches.

A little circle of sky suddenly visible and swifts, hundreds of swifts, and a solitary seagull, pigeons cooing, a reminder that there's a world up there beyond the forest.

The trunks spill out beneath the trees like melted candlewax at the base of a candle. Is that thunder or is it the sound of Bentwaters RAF Base? 'Every little sound just might be thunder/Thunder from the barrel of his gun' – Bob Dylan.

Sleeping giants here too. The trees will listen, overhear you, so you whisper thoughts to yourself. Like being in a great cathedral.

Boles and carbuncles so vast. Huge paunches and bellies on these trees. Birch with shiny bark, rowan, hollies, collapsed and serpentine. Long, leafy wickerwork branches of hollies – males, females, locked in a slow, everlasting embrace. The hoof marks of deer.

In the middle of woods, a bird table sticking out of the bracken. Wrinkled skin and bark. Creeping on all fours to get through, suddenly a lovely clearing, carpeted with brown leaf mould. Shadow, silence.

The bark of a fox. It seems to be getting closer to menace me. Deer tracks and deer droppings.

Here's an oak that's hollowed itself and split right down its trunk – a hermit's home like the one on Lesbos, some ancient lightning bolt having struck it. The presence of ancient thunder.

I emerge into a field of onions, completely lost. Can't even hear a road. A thunderstorm is on the way, rumbling. I stumble away in exactly the wrong direction. I stick to the field of onions – at least I can live on them.

Oaks? Rising up grey in their nakedness, supplicant, reaching to the sky. Leaves and trees so intertwined they mix colours, indistinguishable.

In the darkness I drive past the Rendlesham picnic area, a major site for fornication and adultery. Ragwort everywhere. I'm driving into the thunder, lightning, roof open, rain goes over the top. A dead rabbit.

It is raining, and I gaze out of my study window pondering the drainage system of the white mulberry outside. How many drips, in steps from leaf to leaf, like a waterfall, to the ground? Rain softly decelerated by leaves, so is gentler on the ground. Angle of leaves, spread of roots – umbrella effect.

The young owls tentatively calling in the hedges and on the common in the hour before dawn.

Obscurity is what a writer needs to get on with work well away from the public gaze. Under the glare of lights is the last place you want to be, so, moth-like, you burrow away into some basement or corner of the country, where you can talk to yourself, pace about and think. In the days of letter-writing and the penny post or earlier, it was easier. Forster, in *Howards End*, speaks of a world of 'telegrams and anger' inhabited by the Wilcoxes, and it is the quieter, less accessible world, closer to dreams and sleep, the writer needs. Above all else, though, the writer needs not to think too much about what he's doing.

'If poetry comes not as naturally as the leaves to a tree, it had better not come at all,' says Keats. Running two at a time downstairs you are fine until you start to think too much about what you're doing, and stumble. I blame the Romantics for all this self-consciousness about landscape and inspiration. Wandering lonely as a cloud may be the last thing you need sometimes. Going round the corner for breakfast in a steamy café may be much more like it.

As to my landscape in Suffolk, I chose it originally more than thirty years ago because of its relative obscurity. I pored over maps, deliberately seeking the least-frequented corners, hoping for a ruin drowned in trees a long way down a bumpy track, and that's what I found. Most of my friends lived a hundred miles away in London, and Walberswick and Southwold were relatively quiet little places, where parking a car was not something you ever thought much about, let alone traffic jams on sunny days.

I fixed my house, and chums came to stay, and we had long conversations, walks and bike rides and swims in the river or the sea together. This went on for years.

Walberswick was on the rim of the known world then, and Suffolk itself, or large parts of it, were almost off the map. We were on the margins, *les marginaux*, and we identified with the gypsies in a romantic, starry-eyed way.

Bungay Horse Fair changed all that, and later the Rougham Tree Fair.

'Off the beaten track' and 'unspoilt' were the watchwords. The treks on holiday to find an unspoilt beach. The mad scrambles down to remote coves, simply to get away from other people, to be sequestered, to escape 'the masses' – yet we were socialists.

The myth of the obscurity of the rural *retreat*. Something mawkish about it, hermit's cell, leaving the world. Now people go to ashrams in India, or Tibet, or Hertfordshire. Like the myth of wilderness, the place where no man is. When I was a child, 'No man's land' was what we called the spinney at the bottom of our garden.

No wonder we want to escape our fellow humans when each day we read how nasty they can be to one another. Best to get away from all that in 'the countryside', preferably safely inside a 4WD.

The elver count in the Severn has dropped in recent years as dramatically as the sperm count amongst the young men who traditionally put out in boats from Lydney to harvest them. Nobody quite knows why, but it may well turn out that the two phenomena are really one and the same: something in the water.

27th September

Mum's birthday. Cold and grey at Mellis. Jays, or long-tailed tits, squeaking in the willow trees. Amazing how many birds a tree can conceal.

Mum was a nature girl, always out in the garden, always fiddling with plants, raising a tray of seeds – seed trays were wooden then, knocked up by the thousand out of poplar wood sliced thin for lightness.

28th September

The station car park at Diss is now jam-packed. Impossible to find a space after nine o'clock, and cars parked at odd angles in obvious desperation all over pavements and in assorted corners. Only a few years ago, you could drive up to the station and park in a bumpy, cinder-covered yard, the same one they used for shunting wagons and unloading coal into the coal yard opposite. Parking was free, and there was never any congestion.

There was even a little pub in the yard where you could 'sink a pint' as you waited for the friend you were meeting off the train; and rabbits in the station garden.

After the yo-yo craze, and about a year before the hula-hoop craze, we had a stilts craze.

In fact I think the roller-skate craze came immediately before it, or at least it did in our street. The neighbours, who had been driven half mad by the sound of roller skates clicking over the gaps between the paving stones and the grinding trundle of steel wheels on concrete, were just drawing a collective sigh of relief when the hollow clip-clop of an army of stilts hobbling on the cobbles assailed the net curtains of the neighbourhood.

Stilts-racing, and long-distance stilts-walking, had arrived, and my playmates and I discovered the novel experience of greeting the grown-ups in our street with a lofty, condescending 'good morning' from a great height. Suddenly, we could look down on them. We could even have patted them on the head. For the short-arses like weedy, sickly little Colin, stilts were the perfect answer. Not only could they achieve parity of height by adjusting their blocks a notch or two higher, but they were actually more nimble stilts-walkers, being less top-heavy.

Our suburban stamping ground, for that is exactly what it was, was blissfully free of traffic in those early days of the 1950s. Low brick walls separated the bungalow front gardens along Randon Close and Broadfields from the pavement, and we made use of them as mounting blocks.

My father had made me a pair of stilts in his workshop. You moved the blocks up or down by loosening a thumbscrew and inserting it in a different hole in the pine stilt leg. Beginners started with the blocks close to the ground. The higher you set your blocks, the higher your centre of gravity, and the harder it was to balance. Losing your balance from a great height could be unnerving, and beginners tended to make crash-landings. There was soon an outbreak of grazed knees and elbows in our street. Landing safely was always the problem. The simplest solution was to step off the stilts on to a garden wall. Otherwise, you had to fall forward as gently as possible and step off at the last moment using the stilts in the manner of a pole-vaulter. Good stilts-walkers could pole-vault up on the stilts as well and career off along the street in long, confident strides. Beginners shuffled along, wary of lifting their stilts high enough, and often tripped, with disastrous results.

I am teaching myself to draw, and Alfie obliges each morning at breakfast-time by posing on the kitchen doorstep, just outside the door, in the early sunshine. He adopts a pose, holds very still for five minutes while I sketch him, then shifts into a profile, or turns his great black head to face me, fixing his owlish golden eyes on me as I draw. He likes to be admired, and if I compliment him on his beauty in words, he will purr. The more I word-stroke him, the louder he purrs.

When he scratches under his chin, he looks very superior and snooty. When he licks his paw he looks dainty.

A perfect windy, clear autumn morning. There's a whole lot of buzzing going on. A bluebottle or butterfly on the windowpane, a wasp-faking ichneumon fly whirring and hovering along the beams of my study, looking for a hole in which to tuck himself away for the winter. Alfie sits in a pool of sunshine on the floor, cries out about nothing in particular, then wanders out. Through the open door, the buzz of a chainsaw floats in across the fields.

Listening to the chainsaw, you can tell when they have got

to the interesting bits of the tree: the thicker parts of the main trunk make the saw labour on the way through and modulate the engine note, like a car going up a mountain.

A few hundred yards along the common, one of a pair of old oaks that stand outside Willow Farm has rent itself in two. The split runs straight down the trunk from the top to some three feet off the ground. There's a lot of weight up there, and the leverage of cantilevered branches is increased by the weight of summer foliage, and its action as sails in a wind. It was the leafy sails more than anything else that accounted for the capsize of so many trees in the October storm of 1987, which came early in the autumn, when many of the leaves were still on the trees.

The Suffolk Wildlife Trust, lords of the manor of the common, had wisely decided that the tree should be pollarded before the strong winds of the autumn equinox.

All day the chainsaws buzzed and growled: great thirty-inch McCullochs and Stihls for the main trunk; yet, hearing them from a distance back at home in the knowledge that they were doing good work, they seemed benign, and quite without their usual menace.

Next afternoon my friend and neighbour Ben Box and I began clearing the 'lop and top' of the oak from around its roots and loading logs and branches into my tractor trailer, carting them to each of our wood stacks – ready to be sawn up and split into firewood, or turned into bowls on the lathe, or carved into interesting shapes.

October.

1st October

A sunny morning and door open to my study; a hornet, obviously a queen, came to inspect my lintel for a possible winter quarters. I went out and met her and she looked me in the eye, then flew off. I can hear her now, twenty yards away in an ash tree, with a low buzz: the Marlene Dietrich of the insect world.

Drove down to Cambridge, having spent the morning writing a poem, 'Weasel Words', to Lily Macfarlane [daughter of Robert, then two years old] to go with a posy of lesser teasel seed heads I gave her to sow in the garden in spring. I drove past the finest hedge of traveller's joy (old man's beard) in Suffolk, at the sugar beet factory, disguising the steel mesh and barbed-wire-topped security fence. There's often a subtext to such conservation corporate gestures.

Rob and I talked about Ivor Gurney, a great lover of trees, going mad in England, refusing to go outside at his mental hospital because it wasn't his home county of Gloucestershire.

Jays are harsh and scarifying. Jackdaws' calls sound somehow sweetly reasonable.

Spiders move like lightning, and lightning moves like spiders, legging its jagged way across a night horizon, illuminating the path of a storm.

3rd October

I picked three pounds of elderberries from a single tree by the entrance moat and stewed them to a deep purple-crimson ink. I strained the juice through a sieve and stored the pulp, full of seeds, in a jar, then made a daub-painting from it, using the seeds to represent fruit on a hedgerow.

I raised the three ash trunks off the concrete pad to allow the air to circulate around them. I levered them with crowbars, slid the car jack under each end and jacked them up to the height I needed, then slid blocks of willow underneath as cradles.

4th October

Strong wind driving rain in curtains across the common, waves of spray and spume flecked with the first autumn leaves. Rain and leaves skidding past my window.

Lifting a log yesterday, I found four newts: three palmate, one a baby, and a young great crested newt too, all sleepy and resentful – orange belly in the dark leaf mould.

8th October

Last night a strange thing. I left out a dish of baked salmon fillets I had offered the cats. They had refused the fish on the grounds that I had cooked it with ginger. I covered the dish with a plate overnight, intending to offer it to the vegetable-garden hedgehog. This morning, the plate knocked off, and no salmon. Beside the dish, a dead weasel with a gash in its side and one front leg bitten off. A fox? A badger? I don't think it was a cat, and weasels are fierce fighters. I imagine the gutsy little mustelid standing up on its hind legs to square up to a fox, lashing out with its front paws and losing a limb to nervous snapping jaws. I shall give the creature a decent burial, Barry Lopez-style, and just possibly see if there's a wide-jawed skull in a year or two, but more likely let it rest in peace.

9th October

A fine sunny day and a starry night in the railway wagon, with moorhens and pheasants calling. Moorhens sound like a cork twisting in a wet bottleneck.

Recollections of childhood, sparked by Les Murray on lists of changes.

The bomb shelter on our street, or on the corner of Broadfields outside the Newmens' house, with its cherry tree on the corner and the laurel hedges that I raided to fill my butterfly-killing jars.

Miss Heinz's house on the corner.

Singing lessons with Mrs Gillard, who put her hands on my stomach as I sang.

Skating with Ann Wilks.

Curly at the rec and the sound of the bass booming into my pillow on Saturday nights from the dance band at the Recreation Pavilion.

The sound of roller skates bump, bumping over the gaps between paving stones as we sped downhill, past the railings through which we fed Mr Stimpson's chickens with bread crusts. 'Mum, can we go and feed the chickens?'

Mr Farnborough. Mrs Houlden. Mrs Morongi. Mrs Cracknell and Major Cracknell.

Mrs Cracknell yelling at Hitler to get off her garden fence. 'I can see you, you bugger. You think I can't see you, but I know you're there. Come out of there, you devil!' And she would rattle at the fence with her broomstick. We minded our own business.

The Brabys and Mr and Mrs Hall minded theirs too, the other side. Vivien Braby, a tough, pleasant, somehow Australian sort of girl, who went to Grimsdyke, not Woodridings. I would have gone to Grimsdyke if I hadn't gone to Wellington.

Grimsdyke and Harrow Grammar, had I done well in the eleven plus.

The mud and surfeit of wet bread at Headstone Manor.

Today, sunny and glorious after a misty-sunny dawn (I was in the railway wagon listening to three kinds of owl, all screeching and hooting around me as I tried to sleep, then awoken by the railway-track repair men).

The sheer joy of reusing things that others have discarded, rejects left for dead in skips, or the walking wounded of old chairs or beds in need of repair being auctioned off for a song.

I am interested in the practicalities of life – in clothes, tools, things that serve a purpose with elegance – form or function.

I love craftsmanship. In Morocco I saw people making things everywhere. I have a pair of Moroccan shoes – bought in Tafraoute from a man working in a tiny wooden booth with a modicum of equipment – still going strong. I wear them every day and have done for fifteen or sixteen years. Why don't people make things as good as them in this country, which is so much more technologically sophisticated, or so we are told?

Alison told me a story about shoes. There are three main skills involved in making the uppers of shoes. They are called cutting, closing and finishing. They are taught only one of these skills as apprentices, so that they can't leave and set up as competition. But of course they can join forces with two others and have a business. Hence Freeman, Hardy & Willis.

Also I'm interested in the land, and shoes are our contact with it. Shoes radiate contact with land.

I've had enormous satisfaction and pleasure from good boots that have taken me hundreds/thousands of miles across the land.

It's when I do all my thinking – when I'm walking.

The question about nomadic people is whether their way of life means they are naturally disposed to be nomadic in personal relations too, moving from one friendship to another, even from one wife to another; or does their life predispose them to closer permanent ties? Especially of family? I think the latter. Boots are especially important to nomads. 'If I were in your shoes' – Kazak, Kyrgyz and English. Boots and a good horse, a donkey, a camel – and SHELTER.

Which of us has the more profound relationship with nature? The nomad or the settled, rooted farmer? The Kyrgyz or the Uzbek? In Uzgen in 1990, Kyrgyz and Uzbeks rioted and killed a thousand of each other. Why?

In between stands the transhumant shepherd or herdsman who goes up to the highlands, the alpine meadows rich with flowers, in spring and returns to a lowland homestead in autumn.

The need to travel, to 'get away', is a powerful urge; it has to do with hope and desire and, above all, imagination and the invention that goes with the necessity to improvise from whatever is to hand.

The Tree of Life: the serpentine umbilical cord that feeds

and attaches us to the earth-mother, but from which we also break free at birth. Our roots sustain us, but bind us too.

Satish spoke on Monday night about how trees are sacred to all Hindus, and how Buddha always sat under a tree or trees to teach. Satish sits by the fireside for the same reason. In India the fire is a god and can witness a wedding with no one else present at all. If I say 'You are my lifelong wife' before a fire, this constitutes a binding vow, because it has been witnessed by fire.

I walk about the common with my imaginary medieval friend. 'The ponds are so shallow. Why are they nearly dried out?' he says, amazed at the state of the grass. 'What's happened to all the cowslips and buttercups – and the hay rattle flowers? Where are the clouds of butterflies that used to rise up before the scythe?

'It's so quiet. Where are the voices of the children stone-picking in the fields, where is the birdsong, where are the grasshoppers?'

The elemental nature of a Russian sauna – fire, wood, stone, water, herbs, the heat of the sun released into stone, the small volcano of steam, its thunder, the grumblings and mutterings of the wood stove. The sweat pouring from the body, the pores opening like the stomata of a leaf.

Our own growth – hair, fingernails, like the annual rings of a tree. Autumn – sense of loss, putting extra demands on our capacity for hope.

All of us, I believe, carry about in our heads places and landscapes we shall never forget because we have experienced such intensity of life there: places where, like the child that 'feels its life in every limb' in Wordsworth's poem 'We are Seven', our eyes have opened wider, and all our senses have somehow heightened. By way of returning the compliment, we accord these places that have given us such joy a special place in our memories and imaginations. They live on in us, wherever we may be, however far away from them.

I know a river and a steep valley of dense chestnut woods in the South of France within the golden circle Cyril Connolly described as his ideal habitat, his paradise on earth, roughly encompassing the wooded hills and valleys of the Dordogne, the Lot and the Aveyron rivers.

My particular river and valley, owned purely by right of familiarity and deep affection, are downstream of the little hill town of Souseyrac, high above Saint-Céré, in an almost alpine land of chestnut woods, walnut orchards, hillside beehives and farmyard guinea fowl.

I know a place, down a lane beyond a kink by a half-derelict watermill on an upland road that meanders up to nowhere in particular, where there's a level place at the top of the chestnut wood just wide enough to nudge in the car and make a camp.

Rising up through the trees day and night is a sound that might be a freshening breeze in the leaves, but is the rushing water of what the local people call a 'torrent'. 'Torrent' neatly sidesteps the difficulty of describing in English a gentle enough summer stream that turns into a river the moment there's a thunderstorm in the higher hills or mountains, or into a raging cataract in the spring when the snows are melting.

For several summers I would return to this place in the old Citroën DS Safari I half lived in for July and August, nosing its frog-mouth bonnet into the little clearing amongst the chestnuts, and setting up camp under the shade of an airforce surplus silk parachute that undulated like a swimming stingray at the slightest summer breeze.

Each morning, after a leisurely campfire breakfast, I would descend the steep valley wall through the trees, holding on to saplings and low branches like Robert Frost's 'swinger of birches' until the stream came into view and I could drop down on to the soft leaf mould of the sandy bed of a tiny flood meadow, pooled in warmth as the sun rose up over the treetops.

The moment the meadow lit up, it also filled with insects: delicate blue and green damselflies with barred wings, big emperor dragonflies, flying iridescent shield beetles and wasp-mimicking flies of all kinds, busy in the big white or yellow flowers of the aniseed umbellifers, which filled the place with their Bassett's Allsorts liquorice scent.

This tiny meadow, perhaps thirty or forty yards by twenty, was really a sandy, pebbly island formed by the force of the stream at times of flood, which carried down stones and sandy particles from higher up the valley. The stream swung round it in a wide arc, with rock pools and miniature bays and beaches that immediately aroused all my latent boyhood desires to emulate the water in its playfulness.

For us as children, water, and its close relations mud and sand, always invited play. It turned us all into natural engineers and sculptors. On the beach, we dug canals and channelled the frothing rising tide into our moated sandcastles. Even in the field ditch at the bottom of our garden, we dammed its muddy autumn streams or raced our pooh sticks down its mighty nine-inch flood, clearing the oak leaves and brambles that impeded their progress as diligently as any river engineers.

Here beside the Souseyrac stream, the rising August heat of the morning was an added stimulus to water engineering, and I would set about the construction of a bathing pool, tugging the stones that lay about the island into a natural neck between two rocks, damming it to raise the water level in the pool above so it was deep enough to swim against the stream, making no headway in the powerful current but not falling back either, as trout often do, with so little effort they hardly seem to flex a fin or tail.

Thus, wallowing in my aquatic version of an exercise bike, I could swim for miles, or rather I could chill my blood and clear my hot and bothered head, then clamber out again on to a rock and back into my book. Reading beside the dancing water of a stream, and cooling yourself in it from time to time, must be the summertime equivalent of reading beside a fire in winter, warming yourself by its playful flames, adding a log to stimulate the flow of warmth.

Nobody ever came to this place: the only disturbance was a pair of buzzards mewing overhead, or the occasional rau-cousness of a woodpecker. In autumn there would be the gatherers of chestnuts and mushrooms edging along the contours of the narrow woodland paths; and in winter, the hunters whose red 'Chasse Privée' notices adorned the tree trunks here and there. But in high summer you could be utterly alone beside this pool, glinting with golden flecks of mica, flickering with damselflies. Then, as the sun shifted over the treetops on the western side of the valley, you could climb up to the camp, relight the fire, drink tea and think about supper.

In the motorway café, I think how much I hate those silly diddy little drawings of men and women on the lavatory doors, born out of embarrassment. The horrible blowers you put your hands under, and the obsession with hand-washing. Much more economically done in Kyrgyzstan with the plunger things on posts outside the door.

The poetry is all being efficiently removed, excised, from our land. Where there once stood a magnificent old barn, a rick yard and some half-ruined cow byres and feeding sheds at Withersdale Street, there is now a deeply boring ordinary converted barn. We need ruined barns like we need ruined woods. We need more ruins in our countryside, more evidence of a past, a *living* past. Ruins have a special life of their own.

I walk along the river on the way to Metfield, the bend in

the river near Harleston on the Waveney, and I hear the crackling of a bonfire behind a hedge. It sounds just like heavy rain splashing out of an overflowing gutter in a downpour. Or like the unwrapping of a Christmas present.

Put the hawthorn berries in the fridge for two weeks.

Sebald is a great adventurer – an adventurer in the mind. And he has the genius to take people with him, to keep them as fascinated and curious as he is himself.

On the evidence of history, he is right to be gloomy. After all we've had Cambodia, Kosovo and Rwanda, and many other examples of appalling human behaviour since the Holocaust. There's been no shortage of horrors.

It's hard to drive past the smoking chimney of the sugar beet factory at Bury St Edmunds without involuntarily thinking of far worse things, or the Cambridge pet cemetery on the A505 to Royston – another chimney. Or Golders Green Crematorium.

He is that beetle, he is that hare; like Keats and his 'negative capability'. Sebald clearly believes, like Keats, that writers should whisper results to their neighbour, not shout them from the rooftops. Read Sebald and you can never look at the landscape in the same way again.

At the Village Hall last night, a meeting about the common with Suffolk Wildlife Trust. We discussed the cutting of thistles and nettles at Dam Lane, a modest patch of about one and a half acres, not much trouble to a tractor, but nobody offers to cut it. None of the old sense of commonwealth. Much talk of 'untidiness', of baling up the cut thistles, etc., and burning them! People kept talking about weeds on the common (meaning wild flowers – food plants).

We talked about the recent gypsy invasion – visitors from another planet – an alien landing – and what to do about the mess they left behind – Calor-gas cylinders, old boots, clothes, skirts, plastic bags, fag ends, fire sites, drink cans, etc. I suggested a whip-round in the village to help cover the costs of this nuisance: 300 people × £5 each, say = £1,500, a good contribution towards the total costs, including legal fees. But people said it would be a total non-starter. Better to go and clear up ourselves, they said, and that's even better as far as I'm concerned.

In Puzzle Wood. The whole experience is hugely diminished by the feeling that one has been robbed of any sense of adventure or discovery. You already know what you're going to find. Indeed they tell you on your way in. Also the path is too well worn. In fact I quite liked the smoothness of some of the yew trunks where generations of people have clung on to them for support on the way up or down the steep bits. There should be a law against putting up notices in woods or wild places. One of the notices announced that people found leaving the path would be asked to leave.

Alison and I wandered off the path and immediately lost ourselves in the wood. We made our way towards where we thought the path should be, and it wasn't there. It's easy to lose direction in a wood. Then we heard voices and realized the path was beneath us, almost directly, in a ravine.

The really shocking thing is that nobody said hello to us. Nobody returned our 'good morning' or 'hello', they just stared straight ahead and trudged on. Very odd, out of a dozen family groups or couples we met, only two acknowledged us, and yet there we all were, miles from anywhere, lost in a wood together.

Later, at Spout Farm, we saw the two barns Mr Plant is letting fall down, and the wonderfully down-at-heel green and cream flaking paint on the windows and doors. Either side of the front door of the farmhouse great knotted ropes of ivy root climbed the walls, weaving and knotting themselves into twisted arthritic knuckles of wood. There were even a few bedroom windows missing, and I imagined the family moving from room to room as the house fell down around them and each room became unendurable.

We followed a footpath across fields of cows to the ruined stump of the Great Oak of Newland, once one of the biggest in England. The tree came down in a blizzard in 1955, and its giant stump was still there: a hollowed reef of brown and half-charred oak surrounding a dust bowl created by the cattle. The charring must have been the result of either lightning or a half-hearted attempt to burn out the stump. There was plenty of the original oak left lying there in a ruined heap. I paced out the diameter and it looked like twenty feet (about seventy feet all round). This made the tree incredibly ancient. I stuffed a piece of the great oak under my cardigan and walked back with it to the car. Shameful souvenir-hunting, but why leave it to waste in the field and end up in a farmer's bonfire?

A yard or two from the remains of the old oak a new tree had been planted, presumably about fifteen years after the demise of the original. It was even producing acorns.

The real wages of potters are in the daily silent appreciations of each of their customers as they pour the morning tea from their teapot, or drink coffee from their mug, or eat dinner off their plate. To be thus involved in the daily lives of people who appreciate and admire your work enough to buy it must bring deep pleasure and reassurance. It is a kind of immortality you can enjoy while still living.

The same goes for the woodworker. You are part of the community.

Read biography of Turner – his stroppiness and competitiveness. At the Royal Academy summer show, on varnishing day, Turner would be in there painting over his entry, taking everyone by surprise as all the other painters varnished their work, putting in an indeterminate scene of light, cloud, sea. He would see what competition he had – and *do it better*. Right from the beginning he had fantastic drawing ability. Then he abandoned all that and moved into pure painting and light.

I am sitting at my desk observing a lacewing exploring a piece of yellow paper on the windowsill. It swings its antennae before it with the same corkscrew panache as a drum-majorette swinging her baton as she leads a march. Time passes as I watch this little creature, and a friend telephones and says she thinks maybe it's looking for somewhere to hibernate. She recently purchased a lacewing hibernaculum by mail order. I'm pleased this lacewing will hibernate in my study.

Bang! I'm shaken out of my reverie by my neighbour's twelve-bore. It is dusk, time for the fine cock pheasant that roosts in the hedge that divides our two meadows to ascend into the branches. So he is communing with nature too.

If you shake the branch of an ancient oak above an outspread cotton tablecloth in summer, you will be amazed by the beauty and diversity of the small beings that tumble from amongst the leaves. Some 280 different insects and other small creatures subsist in the bosom of an oak tree, not to mention birds;

hundreds more plant forms – lichens, algae, mosses and fungi – may also find their homes in the same tree. The older and mightier it is, the greater the plant and animal diversity it houses.

Tribes of aphids, bugs, thrips, beetles, moths, flies, butter-flies, wasps, gall mites, spiders . . . The relations between these beings and their host tree is generally ancient and intimate, yet when we walk in a wood or along a hedgerow, it is the oak tree that we see, not the sum total of its many tenants.

Just as popular history has, until recently, tended to focus more on kings and queens, admirals and generals, than on the everyday lives of ordinary people, so natural history has tended to favour the bigger creatures and plants over the smaller ones. Whales, lions, elephants, sharks and anacondas generally command more column inches or television time, while their smaller counterparts in creation are, literally, over-looked.

Often, as an old tree enters the long history of its old age, the insect and the plant life it supports may increase and diversify. Exploring the New Forest recently with a lepidop-terist friend, we discovered a 'goat moth' oak surrounded by clouds of butterflies and hornets feeding tipsily on the rivers of sweet sap that flowed from the labyrinth of tunnels bored into the trunk by the caterpillars of the goat moth. The tree had probably been inhabited for years by successive generations of goat moths returning to lay eggs and parasitize it.

If poetry is about making connections, then Barry Goater taught me poetry. That's what the poetry of earth is. Those first names of moths and butterflies were like the names of first girlfriends. They were emotionally charged with all the potency of an early revelation.

As a naturalist you hope never to lose your virginity, always to be looking with wonder, to remain innocent, wide-eyed.

Night thoughts: the stampede as you enter the Women's Institute market on a Wednesday morning at Eye. You have to be there at 10 a.m. on the dot, else everything's gone by ten past: cakes, jam, loaves, plants, carrots, the lot. Even embroidered birthday cards.

I've been making fig-paintings: gluing the eaten-out fig skins face down on to paper so they look like purple flowers, painted in dense brown/purple oil paint.

I've also made a sculpture of elderberry pips and skins, using the pulp left over from stewing them into ink the other day. I made a little Martello tower in a yoghurt pot, left it to dry, then gently tapped it out and set it on a metal tray in the lower oven to gently bake. I finished it off for half an hour in the top oven, placed it on a square of wood and left it outside in the autumn sunshine to dry. It would have been better in a cone-shaped mould, perhaps wound together in thin card, to make a cone or even a pyramid, but this is a beginning, anyway. I might try black-berries next.

I still do all the things I did as a boy: pick up feathers, roll spiders' webs into balls between my fingers.

All the time you're working with your hands, you are desisting from going crazy.

My mother and I were always at our happiest indulging the outlaw side of our family nature. I still gulp with emotion when I think of our trips north in her open-topped Triumph from Suffolk to the gardens and nursery of Holkham Hall. In autumn, the espalier fruit trees that grew up in the walled gardens were laden with plums, pears and apples that the estate never bothered to harvest. Mum and I would lean innocently against the wall feasting on ripe plums, and always scrumped a few pounds into our ample pockets. 'It's a shame to see good fruit going to waste', we would reason on the way home, sorting the plums into a box of hay.

Another time we stole the stone urn that now stands outside

the kitchen door from a grand house in Hatch End, under demolition to make way for blocks of flats.

David Baldwin and I went out and got Davy Crockett hats made of rabbit skin with raccoon tails down the back and sang the song as we chopped:

> Born on a mountain top in Tennesseee
> The greenest state in the land of the free
> Raised in the woods so's he knew every tree
> Killed him a bear when he was only three
> Daveee, Davy Crockett, King of the Wild Frontier.

We were kings of the wild frontier in Headstone Lane. We had wooden rifles, potato guns and a Vibro catapult (aluminium) that would shoot a boy's eye out at twenty paces.

And we had crystal sets. My crystal set was housed in a plywood box next to my bed, and the wonderful thing about it was that the signal was so weak you could only hear with headphones. This meant hours of pleasure after lights out, beneath the blankets, and I mean Radio Luxembourg and, later on, Radio Caroline. I bought a length of coiled copper wire from the government surplus shop in Harrow and strung it aloft from the gutter pipe to a pole at the bottom of the garden. This brought me Connie Francis, Eddie Calvert's golden trumpet, Danny Kaye, and 'Magic Moments' with Perry Como loud and clear to me beneath the blankets. More importantly, it brought Davy Crockett and 'Tammy'. 'I hear the cottonwoods whisperin' above, / Tammy, Taa-a-my, Tammy's in love,' sang Debbie Reynolds, and I was entranced. What exactly cottonwoods were, I had no idea, but Debbie could sing no wrong and Tammy was in love, and I with Tammy, whoever she was. Cottonwoods and the mountain forests of the wild frontier were elsewhere, a landscape you could only imagine, and therefore a landscape we happily located in our own woods, with ourselves as heroes.

Stroking two cats at once is like bonding both terminals of a car battery. They short-circuit and you get a shock, or a flash, or both.

15th October
Today I sawed off the dead branch of the walnut, leaving three feet at the stump end to lean my ladder on. The wood is still sound. Will it make a bed? Or bed-ends? Could it be turned on the lathe?

Then I loaded the firewood logs from the front into the trailer and hauled them round to the woodshed with the tractor, having unloaded the big oak piece. I threw them all into the woodshed, piling it to the roof with sawn logs, mostly of willow, some ash.

I wish I could give a clear account of exactly how one space in the house feels in relation to another. On a given day, I can do so, but the feelings alter from day to day; are not entirely consistent. From the outside, the state of weather and temperature will have much to do with it. From the inside, my own mood will affect things.

The matter assumes greatest importance when I am deciding where to sleep. I do not always sleep in the same bed. Living alone in a house with several bedrooms gives me a choice. On top of that, there are two other bedrooms outside, one in the shepherd's hut, the other in the railway wagon.

I find I go through periods of sleeping in one place or another. In spring, summer and autumn, my preference is generally to sleep outside in the railway wagon or the shepherd's hut. But in heavy rain both become too noisy; the rain beating on the roof reverberates through the wooden structure and wakes me. Rain also puts me off because I may have to walk through it to the house in the morning, hardly an auspicious start to the day.

Within the house, I have a choice of a big, tent-like bedroom with a high ceiling of oak beams, and a tall sash window at one end facing a green wall of trees, wild hops and a gigantic Paul's Himalayan Musk climbing rose. This can be beautiful and peaceful in spring, or it can feel too big and airy – not containing enough as a sleeping space.

Instead, I can choose the smaller, more intimate bedroom at the opposite end of the house, directly over the warm kitchen and therefore very attractive in winter. But at other times this can feel too unadventurous, too safe, too ordinary a place to sleep, and I crave the mild adventure of sleeping outside in one of the huts or sheds.

At the time of writing, I am sleeping in the railway wagon and enjoying it very much. The location seems to have a direct effect on my ability to sleep soundly. Leaving the house at night after a day's work, I seem to leave behind my cares, and enter a relatively simple world, in which there are only candles, and a small Tortoise stove for heat. In autumn, I take a hot-water bottle out with me.

21st October

The October winds, the equinoctial gales, have arrived and turned the trees into waves of sound, the wind gushing and sighing through them all night. It is through trees that we appreciate and judge the strength of the wind.

To make this much noise, the leaves must still be on the trees, although the wind is busy blowing them off, bashing the branches together to shake them free. It is as if the wind were sent specially to do the job.

In a big wind you wonder whether a tree with many trunks, such as the hazel, or any coppice tree, is designed to withstand wind by dispersing the stress through multiple, slender, streamlined shoots.

I have been out gathering ripe haws along the hedges in Cowpasture Meadow. Six pounds of them sit on the kitchen floor in a yellow bag. After a night of tempest, a piercing clear blue sky and a wild, windy, sunny autumn day. Unable to resist going out and slinging a big yellow Ikea bag incongruously over my shoulder and plucking haws off the bushes as shoppers in the big store pluck goods off the shelves. The rich clusters of berries so red I could scarcely look them in the eye. Plump, squidgy, pulpy things that tumble into the bag as I move my clenched fist down each branch, running it over a thorn here and there and mingling my own blood into the general redness. This is aboriginal work, all right.

Aboriginal people from the central deserts of Australia would be astonished at the richness of our wild fruits here. I imagine them digging dandelion roots and roasting them into coffee, harvesting comfrey leaves for their minerals and medicinal powers, preserving the giant crops of blackberries to live off and nourish them all year round.

I could eat these haws if I wanted to: stew them into a paste and add sugar or honey, or make some sort of savoury gruel – admittedly not very tasty but nutritious. I had soon picked enough to germinate into some seedlings two springs away from now. *Crataegus monogyna* is notoriously hard to germinate because there's such a thick, hard sheath around each seed.

The sheath is designed to break down slowly in the ground, or in the digestive system of a bird, and its thickness is meant to prevent the seed germinating prematurely in the autumn and being killed in winter.

I split more logs, too, and carted them inside while they were good and dry, before the big rains heading here from the west could get at them. Dried by the wind and sun, they sit in a bookend stack at one end of the woodshed.

Here's how time works. When you're young, your mind is running really fast, like a camera over-cranked to produce slow-motion film, so the days and weeks and summers seem incredibly long. When you grow old, the mind slows down, doesn't clock so much sensory stimuli, so the days and years flash by. The same kind of thing happens in a day. Morning time seems longer because your mind is whirring. Evening time goes by faster, because you've slowed down – unless you're being stimulated by lively company at dinner.

I have a bonfire of nettles and dead burdock in the vegetable garden, and the dense smoke is whirling about in the wind.

Making and tending a bonfire is an art. You must first build a small kindling-wood fire in a wigwam shape and get it roaring with red flame and glowing nicely. Then pile the bonfire material on top of it, being careful to leave a way for the air to get in and fuel the fire. What you're doing is constructing a temporary store of vegetation and garden weeds. The heat from the fire is trapped in it, since it is really a powerful insulator, and the whole thing keeps on heating up until at last it spontaneously combusts. A lot of what looks like smoke is actually steam. In other words, the smoke from a green bonfire is largely steam, and a lot of carbon particles too.

I love the way a bonfire whistles and sings as it burns. Sometimes it can sound like a fireworks show.

As the bonfire burns, it will keep on opening up in the middle, like the mouth of a volcano. Your job is to fill that back up with fresh material from the outer edges of the bonfire stack, hooked and flicked in with a pitchfork. Never leave the pitchfork in the fire for more than a split second. Its ash handle is valuable, and very dry and inflammable.

This house is where I've run away to. I ran away from London suburbia, and this is where I landed up. It was the place I imagined must exist all the time as a child, that I knew must be out there, in the country the other side of Pinner Hill and the Grimsdyke, which gave its name to the local elementary school.

As a boy growing up in our tiny half-bungalow in the London suburbs, I longed for some alternative habitat to the cramped two bedrooms, tiny kitchen, bathroom and living room, and my father built it for me at the bottom of the garden. It was a wooden shed, and we called it 'Cosy Cabin'.

23rd October

A noisy autumn afternoon. Minutes after the passing of the three whooping yelling boys and their dogs, the kingfisher is calling from the pond, and a pair of little owls are screeching from the oak on the common. Magpies, squirrels, a wren, a robin. Then a chainsaw strikes up across the field.

It is extraordinary how fastidious bluebottles are. One stands on my desk notepad before me. With its front legs it preens its face, passing them repeatedly over first one eye and then the other. Then it seems to mime handwashing like a little actor playing Lady Macbeth. Next it raises its back legs, always squarely supported on the other four, and preens first its bum, then its wings, one after another, raising the legs in a double-jointed way over its back to reach behind and over each wing. Then it does the handwashing routine with the hind legs, rubbing them together almost as if in disgust at its own filthy ways.

It is strange to think of flies being so fastidious, yet they are, and, considering the places they visit and the things they eat, very sensible they are too.

Today, the trees suddenly look half bare, and leaves are tumbling down everywhere. The crows call hungrily, and birds flit from every branch. The kingfishers are here, fishing a swarming shoal of ten-spined sticklebacks in the moat by the common at the entrance to the garden. Every eight years or so, sticklebacks swarm in this way, perhaps after a summer of plentiful food. Keep some in an aquarium around April/May breeding time and see the males build nests and colour up dark black and deep red. Sticklebacks are the brambles of the ditches, with endless genetic variations between them, and local varieties.

Desmond Morris's first scientific paper, published in 1958, is entitled 'The Reproductive Behaviour of the Ten-spined Stickleback'.

The crow sits in the top of the tree.

28th October

A little dancing troupe of four roe-deer appeared on the lawn, flouncing their white bottoms and skipping like rocking horses from front to hind legs. They circled uncertainly, and took off for Cowpasture Meadow, accompanied by a hen pheasant that flew about them in circles. Men were shooting in the fields beyond my hedges and the lane, and they had probably come for sanctuary. I went out and stood watching them from the field entrance, and the curious thing was that wherever they went, the pheasant went with them, landing and taking off and circling round them like a familiar spirit. They soon decided that I meant them no harm and settled to browsing the clover tips. They were still there an hour later, but no sign of their pheasant friend.

A little flock of fifteen goldfinches rose off the burdock burrs outside Rufus's old cabin as I approached. They reminded me to sow seeds of the lesser teasel in Cowpasture Lane for their greater pleasure. We need more goldfinches here.

29th October
Bike ride – rooks and starlings feeding together on a ploughed field. Nasty orange weed-killed grass. If they're going to ban smoking in public places, how about banning pesticide spraying in the open country?

Can growing hay for horses be regarded as an agricultural activity? We no longer use horses for ploughing, and we don't eat horses in Britain. Isn't keeping horses, including racehorses, a branch of recreation? Harvesting hay from a common for sale to horse-owners, whose sole use of the horses is to ride them recreationally about the lanes, is not really an agricultural activity.

On the other hand, harvesting hay for cattle is an agricultural activity, consistent with the traditions of a common.

If recreation, rather than agriculture, is to be the new 'harvest' of our common, then surely we should be taking into account the needs of nature as a prime 'user' of the common. It means adjusting our thinking about the constituency of the common beyond the purely human. The old agricultural practices left plenty of slack for the plants, insects, birds and other animals to exercise what you might call their natural common rights. Under the traditional view, the owls and foxes exercised hunting and fishing rights over the common. The bumblebees exercised their right to gather pollen. Certain butterflies and moths exercised their long-standing right to lay eggs on particular plants or trees and their caterpillars exercised their right to forage on them. Skylarks exercised their right to rest undisturbed amongst the grasses of the common. Frogs, toads and newts had ancient rights to breed in the ponds and to enjoy unobstructed passage, often over quite long distances, to and from these ponds to their terrestrial feeding and hibernating grounds.

We see all these sorts of activities going on in places like the African Serengeti on television, and we admire the spectacular examples offered to us, and the harmony of nature. Yet we can observe a process and a web of activity just as marvellous right here on our common, under our noses, if only we will take the trouble.

November.

I went to exercise my rights to gather watercress from a pond on the common this morning. A brilliant clear, windy, sunny dawn, and I filled a small knapsack with cress and brought it home. When I washed it in the sink, and then left it floating in the full sink, little slugs and worms, perhaps nematodes, appeared on the bottom. It would be interesting to put the pond mud under a microscope.

Fire – bathwater. At Steward's Wood they had a bath poised over a wood fire to heat up the water. Trouble was they were in danger of being cooked, as cannibals are traditionally represented cooking missionaries (a thoroughly sound idea).

6th November

The swarming shoal of ten-spined sticklebacks is still active in the front moat by the common. The kingfishers are delighted. Much sounding of their little piping hunting horns. 'What time the grey-fly winds her sultry horn' (Milton).

The foundation of a first-class talent is eyesight – perception. The first-class writer always has first-class eyes. Those who observe quickly and vividly hold us with the details they see. Their stories have a flow that carries the reader.

The rare first-class writer has, in addition to keen sight and hearing (it may be because of them), feelings or emotions that are equally keen.

8th November

I sawed up some of the kindling wood in my dry hedge by the big willow beside the common this morning. It was satisfying slicing through the laid and dried boughs, turning them into useful kindling and firewood, so no part of the trees I had cut two years before was to be wasted. Making bonfires of perfectly useful kindling wood for the sake of convenience is as stupid as driving an SUV because it wastes valuable fuel resources. Frittering is something we can no longer afford.

A robin came down and joined me as soon as I shut down the din of the chainsaw, hopping about the sawn wood, pecking up grubs as I loaded logs into a wheel-barrow. It is good to feel the blessing of a wild bird trusting you like that.

Starfish of orange peel drying on the stove top. The skin of the outstretched arms tautening as it dries, filling the room with the aroma of my mother's Seville orange marmalade stewing in our kitchen.

9th November

Tonight in the Sunday-night stillness of my study, I listen to the buzzing of an ichneumon fly. Where does it get its energy from? How can it possibly keep on flying and flying round the room as interminably as it does? It comes to rest close to the black windowpanes, settling on an upright oak beam that seems to hold some fascination for it. It has returned again and again to hover around the entrance to a peg hole and even to enter it and explore inside. Perhaps it thinks of hibernating there. But for now it rests for twenty minutes at a time, almost camouflaged by the nutty brown of the beam, and just ruminates. It chews its mouth parts and preens its antennae, then rests motionless on the oak, then rubs its front legs together as though washing its hands.

The strange thing about ichneumon flies is that each time there seems to be just one individual buzzing and droning about the room. Eventually it lands on the windowpane; I open the window for a moment, and it flies out. Five minutes later there's another ichneumon fly in the room, and I go through the same rigmarole all over again. And so it goes, as though the same fly knows a secret door into my study and keeps sneaking back.

Outside on the window there's a moth, a small olive moth with a row of darker spots like hemming stitches along the lower border of each wing. Its plump little body is pressed against the glass, perhaps for warmth, and the creature has a wing span of just over an inch. It is a cool night, but not frosty, and there is no wind or rain.

The ichneumons keep coming in here, keep bumping into the same spider's web and getting hopelessly entangled before freeing themselves at the last moment as the spider dashes towards them to give them a lethal bite.

Watching this fly and its continual buzzing, I realize all insects are living batteries. They charge themselves up on sunny summer days, then fly about discharging that energy.

10.05 p.m. Now he's stopped for a tea-break and a wash and brush-up. First the front legs and face-washing, then tip up the other way and rub the hind legs together, and reach them back over the abdomen and slide them up under the wings to give them a dusting down. Then wring the back legs together again as if in anguish, which it probably is, because a spider's web is a hard thing to shrug off once you've got one stuck to you.

An ichneumon is a big beefy fly dressed up to look like a wasp or bee. This one looks like a honey bee. It's the right size and shape, and it's even got a furry top to its head. And of course it sounds right too: it buzzes like a bee. It doesn't actually sting, though, because it's a fly. And its absolutely harmless. It wouldn't even hurt a fly.

I think you can understand a lot about a person from their taste in wood – especially furniture – chests of drawers, e.g. the featureless hardwoods of the 1920s.

10th November

Today I swam (thirty lengths) from 1.45 to 2.15, worked on TV outline of *Touching Wood* and finished carving my cherry sculpture for Viva [Pomp]. I carved out the centre with the chainsaw, smoothed the front surface with a sander, placed the piece on a willow log out on the concrete pad where I was working and filled the hollow with wood shavings. I set fire to these and they kindled immediately and flared up, flaming vigorously and smoking, the hollow acting as a chimney. The fire was so quick and fierce that, before I knew it, it was licking around the lips of the hollow and beginning to char the front surface, which I had meant to remain unsullied in pale contrast to the blackened interior. I doused the fire at once with the watering can and examined the steaming cherry wood. The chimney fire had produced just the right effect, and all I had to do was clean up the front surface with fine sandpaper and rub in a liberal dose of linseed oil on the flat cross-section of the trunk and on the convex outer surface, clad in beautiful deep red-brown flecked bark.

I was delighted with this sculpture and felt my long-distance apprenticeship to David Nash was going pretty well. I had followed his principle of charring the interior, thus emphasizing the hollow, and accentuating the pure line of the aperture running gracefully from top to bottom of the upright wood.

None of this was in the least original, but it felt profoundly satisfying to be doing the work. The making itself was pure pleasure, and I felt that as long as I was always honest about the origins and inspiration of the piece in the work of David Nash, it was perfectly legitimate as a form of five-finger exercise.

I drew the piece in charcoal from the burnt spinney, and then wrapped it up in black cartridge paper for Viva's fortieth birthday present.

11th November

It's mid November and crickets are still singing outside the kitchen door at Mellis, and bumblebees are still visiting the nasturtium flowers.

12th November

I have a hedgehog in residence beside the Aga. It's a young one, no bigger than my outstretched hand, and I found it in a stupor, exposed beside my track in broad daylight. Young hedgehogs are vulnerable to this kind of inexplicable malaise at this time of year; lacking enough body mass to withstand sudden cold, they seem to run low on blood sugar and grow torpid. This leaves them dangerously exposed to attack by winter-hungry crows, or magpies, or hawks. In any case, once they have grown this cold, they often simply lose the ability to get up and look for food and water, and decline further into death.

I brought this animal inside and placed it beside the Aga, where it curled up and slept for hours before stirring and eating some cat food. It then drank vigorously for six minutes, emptying a large dish of water, then slept again, creeping inside a cardboard box of dry leaves of ash and mulberry. The cats take little interest in it, as they're quite used to sharing their feeding bowl with wild hedgehogs. The little thing has gradually gained strength over the last twenty-four hours and has explored the kitchen, eaten more food and retired into the box again, where it noisily goes about its occupational therapy with the leaves.

There's something medieval about a hedgehog: the scavenging peasant of the undergrowth, the hedge bottom. What we love about them is their vulnerability, which they share with human babies: the way they curl up in that foetal ball, shielding the soft furry underbelly.

I'm trying to work out what that sound is, exactly, inside the box. Is it chomping, the squeaking of one mandible against another? The animal is an indefatigable trencherman or woman.

A brilliant sunny day, and an excellent full night's deep sleep from 12.30 to 8.30 a.m., in the big room, scented with stored apples, early sunlight slanting in.

In a dark Norfolk lane driving at speed behind Adam Nicholson in his VW, the brown toasted beech, oak and chestnut leaves swirling and tumbling in the slipstream of three cars as we whiz along beside wide verges and hedges. This is how roads are meant to be. No mean farmers pinching bits of land.

We go through North Creake, past endless brick and flint walls with brick copings beautifully made by craftsmen. Walls, endless, five feet tall, fine verges where I've camped in the past. Out through Holkham, past the hall, and still the flint wall continues, the beechwoods and the fallow deer within.

'As I walked out one midsummer morning' is how Adam sees my journey. He sees the interludes at home as being OK too. In a way, you end up writing about home when you travel away like this.

18th November

I set out up Clay Street in Thornham Magna this afternoon, in quest of a little medieval meadow full of ancient pollard oaks. It was, I had been told in strictest confidence by a local tree-detective, a pheasant park in miniature, a tiny wood pasture, and so it proved.

Clay Street is a narrow no-through road branching away from the Thornham Horseshoes between old hedges of ash, maple and blackthorn with an old pollard oak every fifteen or twenty yards, and patches of the shocking pink fruits of the spindle tree.

Every now and again I passed a pink thatched cottage, with a modest garden, two or three apple trees, and a makeshift garage and a range of tin sheds slanting towards oblivion. Nearly all of them had the builders in. A white van, a cement mixer, a pile of Durox building blocks and the beginnings of an extension or a porch were the only evidence of activity. Not a sign of anyone actually at work, not even Radio Norfolk to break the silence.

At the corner of two fields and the road, a digger had been excavating a pond. There are so often ponds at the intersections of fields here in Suffolk, and it was good to see how sensitively the big machine had been eased in amongst the trees that fringed the pond; how it had deftly scraped out only the leaf silt, leaving the hard clay-bottom intact.

A multiple covey, or an extended covey, of dozens of partridges whirred up like an aeroplane the other side of the hedge and dived straight ahead, flying two feet off the ground. They landed, stood about long enough to realize I was still gaining on them and broke into their comical run, eventually taking off with their usual reluctance.

The country began to roll a bit just here, and the dark cushions of ancient maple and sloe hedgerows snaked and curved away downhill, following the classic undulations that signal old field boundaries. I had turned off Clay Street into a green lane signposted 'The Six-Mile Loop', passed another shadowed pond winking out from a canopy of trees and turned left along a banked field boundary. The line of massive pollard hedgerow oaks, and sheer bulk of bank and width of ditch, suggested that this may once have been the boundary of the medieval park at Thornham. The trees were hollow and black with ivy. Out of the shaggy log of one of them flew a little owl.

Rabbits had made their burrows amongst the huge roots in the sandy, dry earth inside the hollows, and a beefsteak fungus jutted out of the trunk.

I entered a wood of overgrown ash and old hazel coppice bursting densely from old stools and followed the rides on a course that curled back towards the road behind the cottage and gardens that occasionally fringed it.

I ducked through the hazels into a clearing and saw the first of the old coppice oaks. It was a giant, superbly misshapen, its trunk a cluster of carbuncles and its branches withering and bursting forth at the same time. It was alive and dead, young and old, all at one. There were fourteen trees grouped about no more than an acre and a half of tangled blackberry and nettle jungle. Two or three oaks had collapsed, splitting themselves apart under the weight of their own crowns and falling outwards in several directions. Another had simply died on its feet, standing straight up like a ghost, but more petrified than rotten, riddled with beetle burrows and woodpecker drills.

Seized by a nerdish urge to measure and to count, I spread out my arms and flung myself flat against the trunks of these oaks, hugging them close to my bosom and stretching out my fingertips as far as they would go, then worked around the tree back to the point where I had begun. Each tree was just over three arm spans in girth five feet off the ground. My arm span is a fraction under six feet, so the trees are eighteen feet in girth or 216 inches. Applying the unreliable method of a half-inch to every year for a tree in a wood (or an inch a year for free-standing trees) they would be at least 430 years old. That would place them around 1570. Oliver Rackham says he knows of pollarded oaks in Epping Forest of only fifty inches in girth that are known to be at least 350 years old. The trunks of pollards grow more slowly because the tree is concentrating on growing its topmost boughs: doing what it is meant to do. The trunk is simply the body of a roman candle, shooting out leafy fireworks every spring and summer.

Beyond these oaks, the kitchen lights of one of the thatched estate cottages winked out as dusk began to fall. The cottage had a lawn and an apple tree still festooned with pale yellow fruit, unharvested, and more windfalls all over the lawn beneath. This was a sight you would never have seen in the past, any more than pollard oaks left uncut; such things were the staples of the lives of working people.

This place, with its oaks, is still known as 'the meadow' and would have been a miniature wood pasture, with sheep or a cow or two grazing beneath the oaks, and perhaps some pigs let in to eat the acorns.

I searched for acorns to plant and propagate descendants of these trees but found none. They must all have been gathered already by squirrels and mice.

Walking back down Clay Street, I chased the same whirring partridges and passed more bright pink spindle trees.

Great ropes of ivy, six inches thick, clambered up the wayside oaks, and they seemed none the worse for it. On some trees the ivy had been sawn through to kill it, though it sometimes managed to mend itself and grow back together.

I passed barns converted to houses with the regulation full-length glazing, floor-to-eaves, affording too public a cross-section of life inside, as though the inhabitants were living on the set of a rural *Big Brother* show. These barns are always weather-boarded and creosoted a uniform black, and they always have crisp shingle drives and open-fronted pseudo-cowsheds as garages. Water butts are in vogue too, and the barn I passed on Clay Street contained a long-legged Persian cat, too domesticated to be allowed out of doors.

Most of these barns used to be prime habitats for bats until converted. A recent survey amongst the barn conversions of Hertfordshire showed that, in spite of the fitting of the regulation bat lofts, access holes and the rest of it, as required by the planners, the bats have disappeared from 75 per cent of them.

The gamekeeper, patrolling the stubble fields round the woods and copses in his Toyota pick-up – sinister, impersonal, detached, alienated from nature.

The hedgehog is male (it has no discernible apron) and, as it fumbles about furtively prospecting for a hibernaculum amongst the horded Tesco bags under the butcher's block by the kitchen sink, it sounds like a boy masturbating in a dormitory after lights out.

19th November

Hornets. All through the late summer and autumn they kept coming. Each night successive waves of bombers droned in across the garden, targeting the study window in front of my desk. I had to remember to close it before switching on any lights. They went straight for the light, flying in down the beams that reached out into the autumn evening mists, and picketed the windowpanes. They were inches away, the other side of the glass but still dauntingly big, their striped bodies throbbing with energy, wings never still. Close up, I watched as they demolished whole leaves and stems of the jasmine plant, each insect eating its way methodically down its chosen stem, from tip to base.

Up in the roof, their nest kept growing like a giant brain, lobes ballooning ever higher into the apex of the roof behind the chimney, where the hornets squeezed in and out through a crack between the bricks.

I notice the difficulty I have in stepping off the paths across the common and treading my own new one. There is almost a force field that guides my steps. But, in doing so, I can express myself in the landscape: leave my mark. But it raises the question of how paths are formed in the first place. This path along the common that passes in front of my house is relatively recent. I would say it originated no more than eight years ago or even less. It is one of the ways people go towards Cowpasture Lane.

Recently, more and more people have come to live in our village, converting barns or even building new houses. In my own stretch of the common, which runs just over a mile, the population has risen since I first settled here from twenty-nine (including children) to sixty-five.

I can lie in my warm bed upstairs and watch the pheasants waking up in their roost in the spinney at one end of my house. The old cock pheasant roosts there – he patrols the lawn – and today it is not until 7.30 that he eventually flies down to the field to feed. He has spent twenty minutes rousing himself out of a ball of feathers into the shape of a pheasant. It has been a sharp frosty night, and the twigs are sugared with frost.

To my mind, a microscope, or a telescope, or a pair of binoculars, are all far better presents for a child than a TV set.

A microscope gives you access to a whole world of amazement and wonder.

21st November

A sharp, sugaring frost. The mulberry is at its best in November when at last it undresses itself. It does a sort of striptease before my study window, lightly letting go its leaves in a light breeze that seems to touch only this one tree after the stillness of the frosty night. The leaves float down in twos and threes, or just a single leaf at a time.

The glory of the mulberry at this moment of the year is in its pool of fallen leaves: pale yellow softened by pale green and buff (the last from beneath the canopy). The pool is a little sea, choppy with leaves. (Each leaf is a wavelet.)

Mulberry leaves feel tough and gleam like oilskin. They are dull green when they fall from the tree, then turn to chestnut brown as they oxidize. Each leaf is serrated subtly and evenly with little millimetre sawteeth, and the veins are the tributaries of a river, whose delta leads down to the stem.

Elderberry leaves pale almost to white except for their veins, which blush a deep crimson as though animal or human arteries, filled with coursing blood.

Last year I made a maze in the mulberry leaves to celebrate the birth of a little girl – for her first visit here, a labyrinth.

Why are park-keepers so keen to sweep up leaves? They

are the glory of autumn and surely would feed the ground if left alone to be drawn underground by earthworms and composted?

All the leaves are falling this morning after such a frost. It has loosened them, frozen and cut off the flow of sap, made each stem brittle.

A pair of crows come to the bullace tree on the common before the house and balance on twigs too slender to bear their weight to eat the plums, translucent pearls of pink and yellow, softened and ripened by the frost, their sugars concentrated now. Magpies follow them, then a dozen black-birds, a pair of song thrushes. A wood pigeon on the hawthorn after haws.

The hazel is dropping its leaves too, shivering now and then in a breath of slightest breeze. Leaves come to earth like birds to a field for grain, or grubs.

Why don't all the leaves come down at once?

The fun of scuffing leaves as you trudge through them as if through a snowfall, the woodland floor turned to a palette with each tree at the centre of its particular colour. (Turner's palette.)

As the leaves fall away from them, the naked branches reveal their lichened beauty. The pool of fallen leaves is a mirror, reflecting the tree as it has been: the whole canopy in two dimensions. Only the skeleton of the tree is left to represent the third dimension.

That is what trees give us: the third dimension in our landscape.

Left alone to cloak the woodland floor, leaves accumulate layer by layer over the years into a deep crust of leaf mould. Walking, or clambering, through old beech or chestnut woods in France and Poland, I have sometimes fallen through the leaf crust and dropped many feet into a soft drift of leaves.

These leaf drifts often fill hollows or old quarrying sites for limestone or chalk.

I go for an early swim and notice the fine old ash pollards on the road back to Thrandeston, and on Thrandeston Green. They need cutting too, but who will do it? I must make a map of Mellis pollards. All need attention to survive. And why not start new pollards too, as I have with my pollard willows?

25th November
Curious effect of a sky in two minds about itself. One half, the eastern, dirty grey and smoky with low cloud; the other glowing palely white and washed-out blue, falling away to the south and west. Then rain comes, straight down through the bare remnant leaves, falling on dead leaves.

I talk on the phone to Peter Randall-Page on Dartmoor. He is racing to get his Eden Project sculpture of Cornish granite finished by June. As usual, nobody realizes quite how much work goes into such things. He had a giant lathe built to turn them, but it took the engineer nine months to make. Now it is working well. Meanwhile, he is making a new square in the middle of Cambridge near the Corn Exchange, and waiting for the stone he went to New England to select for his memorial to a Mohican American Indian at Southwark Cathedral.

The peanut dispensers hanging on the plum tree outside my window are busy with tits and greenfinches. I notice there are more sparrows this year. They come in flurries with the wind.

People now are constantly thinking in terms of artificial re-creation of natural places. They want owl-boxes instead of old barns or half-derelict hollow pollards. They want to plant hedges instead of just letting old ones be. They must plant trees and accelerate their growth with plastic sheaths like greenhouses, and weedkiller round the roots. They must plant whole woods, rather than letting them find their own way into existence.

A hectic, strange week at Mellis, returning on Sunday night, late after Steve Ashley's gig, driving home with Harvey Brough to find the house in darkness from the gales and a power cut. On Sunday morning during the height of the gale I had to saw my way out along the track to get out to buy an *Observer*.

A big dead ash tree came down on the common and I decided to go and cut it up for firewood: 30 ft tall, 90" girth, 2'6" diameter of trunk and 148 annual rings, the tree's history of drought and plenty, warm years and cold ones, all there in the rings. I sawed up from both sides and split the big logs so I could lift them on to the trailer, then took a scaffold board and rolled them up like cheeses. I stored them in a row against a fence, and made a tin roof over my store. Also filled up the woodshed to the roof.

Wild is an absolute: you can't have wildish, or semi-wild.

Rob, chairing the seminar in Cambridge, says that everything I've said tends towards diffidence, an abrogation of the self or selfhood. I reply that 'here lies one whose name was writ in water' – that poets, in Keats's view, have not any real individuality. I should have mentioned Lawrence and self-conscious: his detestation of it as something that de-educates children and militates against spontaneous creativity. The swimmer, dissolving himself in water, immerses himself in the natural world and takes part in its existence.

There is all the difference between the twitcher going to see the bird and ticking it off in his book (this is all to do with the twitcher, not the bird, a reality) and the poet/swimmer, who allows things to swim 'into his ken' – the naturalist or poet as passive more than active. 'We should rather be the flower than the bee' (Keats).

A journey and its serendipity.

You look back on where you have gone and realize that unconscious connecting forces have been at work. Or were they acting somehow from outside? Are you following some natural pattern you instinctively recognize but at a pre-conscious level? Did I know, when I went to Hell Gill, that it would represent such primeval, atavistic forces? Such life and death, being born and descending back into the earth. But then, how did I find my way there at all? Purely by chance, apparently. And yet I did have a deep desire to go underground, to follow water underground.

All the most sacred places are secret; therefore you don't want to have a website publicizing them. I swam in countless places without revealing where they were. This is the advantage of writing a novel. When I wrote *Waterlog* I approached it like a novel.

A few years ago I found myself in Aldeburgh, living in a seaside house and making a film about Auden's and Britten's *Paul Bunyan*: six young opera soloists singing about trees and woods.

I remember the stirring of spring in the forest, evoked in the opening music in the woodwind. It is billed modestly as an operetta, but I think it is a wonderful work, because in it we hear the stirring of the spring in Britten himself. It is his first attempt at writing opera, and he is doing it with one of the great poets of the twentieth century, Auden. The opera got me thinking about woods and trees, and what wood people we all are.

The carved oak angels in the roofs of Blythburgh Church, and at March in the Fens, and along the road in Southwold, are watching over us, like the trees themselves. They are our guardians.

At Christmas people usually perch a fairy or an angel on the Christmas tree's top. But perhaps all trees have an angel in their branches somewhere.

When the wind blows and the elms go, we feel a great sense of loss. Trees are the guardian spirits of the land, therefore angels.

27th November
What are a cat's whiskers for? Looking at Millie, I wonder what the 'eyebrow' whiskers, like Salvador Dali's upward-reaching ones, are for? Are they redundant relics of earlier evolutionary advantage? Or gene-linked characteristics like the cockerel's comb?

Stationery, the tools of the trade, never fails to excite most writers. I say most because when I wandered, swooning with delight, through the Pencil Museum at Kendall in the Lake District with Richard, he was less enthralled than I – but nevertheless humoured me most generously.

A stationery stall in the Queen's Crescent Market in Kentish Town is one of my favourite haunts. Whenever I travel abroad, I buy notebooks and interesting pens.

In a little cupboard of a room next door to my study, I keep a stash of ink bottles, pencils, notepads and folders. My friend Min knows a special shop in Museum Street where she can still buy old-fashioned dip pens and brass nibs of all sizes to fit them. This is about as near as we get, these days, to the quill, but I have made quills and used them, if briefly, in the past. Swan or goose feathers do best for this.

My favourite two pens are my Rotring Art Pen, and the Lamy, whatever that means, bought for me as a present at Melbourne Airport.

A late-afternoon walk in the big black overcoat with a stratum of mist settling above the common, severing the trees and bushes, pale, soft white line decapitating the trees. I took photos as the sun went down, then gathered hawthorns off the cow-worn thorn tree in the cattle dip on the way to the stone bridge.

An amazing sight across the valley of the Pountney Stream: Michael's tractor towing a muck-spreader disgorging clouds of smoke and fire from the hot steaming dung it was flinging on to the field. A horizon of wild steam against the silhouette of the dark wood at Burgate.

The cow-worn hollow under the thorn tree: dark loam scattered with flints.

29th November
Last night, blood-curdling sounds of a squirrel either fighting another or, more likely, being carried away by a cat or some other predator. Its gurgles, gratings and screeches gradually grew fainter and more distant, until they disappeared into the night wind.

My early life as a trespasser in the farmland on the fringes of the suburbs laid the foundations of the Robin Hood in me. We learnt to live lives in the woods and fields like rabbits constantly on the alert for signs of Mr Stimpson, the farm bailiff, or any of his henchmen. He was the Sheriff of Nottingham, and we were Robin Hoods. We crept about in the corn, or hid in the fringes of the wood intently observing Stimpson's movements about the farm. We studied the patterns and rhythms of his day. We learnt to recognize the excitement of his poultry when he fed them and knew he would be sufficiently distracted at such moments for us to make a bolt across the green field to the cover of the trees, which had a carp pond at their centre.

I remember the day we first discovered the carp in that pond. It was like finding pieces of eight glinting out of the green depth.

30th November
Tonight at 8.15 p.m. in pitch darkness, a goldcrest suddenly appeared on the study window. It clung to the window frame and looked alarmed, but stayed there, pecking at the odd insect, then flew away after a couple of minutes, back into the windy night.

December

Fire. It begins with a slender, splinter stick of poplar, a matchstick. How many matchsticks are there in a single poplar?

When wind blows through poplars, they sound like a match alighting when you strike it.

To light a fire, you start from small beginnings. Good firelighters understand small beginnings. Kindling, what a pleasant word it is – how warm and friendly.

Writing about building the house. My inky notebooks of the time are smudged with brick dust and thumbed with grimy hands. The record drawings of roof trusses, lengths of nails, calculations of moments of force: all the stuff I wish I had paid attention to in Physics. The engineering I had needed to learn. A crash course, if that's the word, in engineering.

6th December

Pockets. Boys pick up odd things – a snail, a pebble, a leaf, a dead beetle, a chrysalis, a bit of sheep's wool on a fence – and their pockets soon come to resemble birds' nests. The contents of the pocket have no intrinsic money value, but they do have great sentimental value to their owner. They become a microcosm of the local landscape, of the boy's habitat and haunts.

The boy's pocket is marsupial. It is close to a secret drawer – or a secret safe, such as the biscuit tin I had buried in the garden full of my fossils and even pocket money. The biscuit tin was buried under a false roof of moss, earth and dead leaves.

Is Larkin any good? Try this: 'It deepens like a coastal shelf.' Or try this: 'the moon thinned / To an air-sharpened blade'. What about Ted Hughes? 'Deep as England' (the word 'deep' again). 'The hare strays down the highway / Like a root going deeper.'

We are always talking about the visible, the tip of the iceberg, tree, but what of the *roots*?

On a frosty morning, apples shining in the sun on the bare

tree by the roadside and the gleaming litter of apples beneath.

The harrow patterns on the frosty fields. A solitary blackbird begins a spring-like song in a tree. A man is in his bath behind a massive wall of cypresses in the row of cottages, singing. 'That'll be the Day' by Buddy Holly, over and over again. Man and blackbird. 'That'll be the day when I die.' That is the line he keeps singing.

The hazel handle round which I wrapped my kite string and unwound it as my yellow box kite rose and swooped in the wind. The hazel handle became smoother and even smoother, its freckled bark polished to a perfect mirror that reflected the sun. And it became a musical instrument as it hummed and thrilled to the vibrations of the taut kite string.

There was nail-biting, and the bitter aloes they painted on the nails to stop it. Then stuttering. Dreading my turn to read in class. As it came round to me, I would be searching ahead in the prose for the hurdles, which all stood out as if in orange headlights: '*the* this', '*the* that'.

I arrive chez Ronnie down the hollow-way track that skirts the steep brown side of a ploughed hill at around 3 p.m. Ronnie's washing is on the line and a couple of plastic bowls and a biscuit tin full of wooden pegs are beneath it on the lawn. The washing line has been stretched between a pair of old apple trees.

You go up a couple of stone steps and walk straight into the living room, with a low beamed ceiling and fire glowing in the open wood-stove. To the right of the inglenook, where the copper used to heat the household water, is a neat stack of split firewood five feet high. Ronnie splits it himself, and enjoys the exercise with the axe. Two spotted white cats drape themselves on the back of armchairs as Ronnie goes upstairs to fetch yet another book he has just written or edited.

He tells me about the Singing Men of the church bands in Thomas Hardy's time, and Hardy's story of how, when one of the Singing Men was buried, the others wanted to stand round his grave singing, but the vicar forbade it because it was too wet and stormy, so the Singing Men went back at night after the burial and sang anyway.

Ronnie is always full of stories like this, squirrelled away in his head: how Keats went to see the publisher he shared with Clare, although the two never met, and, finding the publisher out and a sheet of paper on the table, wrote a note on the back of one of Clare's poems. How the gamekeepers always kept a gibbet on which they hung the dead bodies of the animals they killed: weasel, stoat, magpie, kestrel, sparrow hawk, squirrel. Moleskins were collected to sew together and make moleskin waistcoats.

Ronnie says much nonsense is talked about Suffolk houses having low ceilings because the people were shorter in those days. Actually, it was about the availability of trees and their natural proportions – they dictated the form or proportions of the house.

People working outside in the fields all day weren't at all bothered about having windows in their house. A view was the very last thing they wanted after eighteen hours on open fields. They wanted to creep inside somewhere warm and comfortable and sit down to a meal and go to bed. There was no time for gazing out of windows.

18th December

A tortoiseshell taxies up the windowpane, flexing its wings as if seeking the optimum angle for flight. The little insomniac should be fast asleep, immersed in hibernation, its metabolism slowed to the point of torpor. Instead, its colours are vivid with life, antennae raised straight, and the fur on its back luxuriant. Now it suns itself beneath my anglepoise. Amazing to see such beauty of summer in winter.

Cycling out this brilliant morning, I think the bike ride is like boring a geological sample through the strata of local Suffolk. First, I encounter a walker, who returns a surprised 'Good morning', clearly caught off guard by my salutation, and not at all sure about the correct form. Then I pass an old boy in a car who slows down for me and we exchange waves. His is a proper Suffolk wave: lingering, with the forefinger raised as if for the peak of the cap. Then I pass another cyclist coming the other way. I say 'Good morning' and she just keeps looking straight ahead with no sign of acknowledgement even. I very nearly turn round and remonstrate, I feel so angry and offended at such manners. Most of the people I see are armoured in some way – the people in their enormous 4WD armoured vehicles.

The little shadow of each fallen leaf across the common. The old hawthorns, pruned by the cattle to look like orchard apples. The single clouds hanging like balloons.

The shadow of a hedge thrown across the road like a rood screen (opposite Burgate Church).

Reading *Howards End* under the elm, you come to see more and more what isn't there but once was. You see the ghosts of once great trees that have fallen. You understand how Forster felt when he spoke of the 'red rust' of suburban sprawl creeping across the countryside. Now its equivalent is the creeping disease of unsociability. People have brought the manners of Oxford Street with them to the country and look at you oddly if you greet them in a lane or out walking on the common.

It's not hard to imagine a wildly dancing woman into the ash tree that embraces the house. The way the wind silvers her hair in the backs of the leaves. The way the whole tree sways and bends with the wind's passion.

Sometimes an author and his title become one and the same thing in your imagination. So it is with Eric Rolls, whose Australian classic *A Million Wild Acres* tells the history of the Pilliga Forest in northern New South Wales through the hundreds of stories of its Aboriginal natives, settlers, wood-cutters, timber-getters and outlaws. The writer himself has come to seem a million wild acres, filled with histories and natural histories, so deeply in love with his land that he has become the land. Like a shaman, he has taken on its skin.

I was introduced to *A Million Wild Acres* a few years ago when my Sydney friend Tony Barrell sent me a copy with a note saying 'I think you'll like this.' I certainly did. I have never really stopped reading the book since then. It has been a never-ending source of pleasure and fascination.

Eric Rolls writes his history of the Pilliga Forest in a series of anecdotes and portraits that accretes bit by bit into a whole picture. Les Murray calls Rolls's technique 'pointilliste' and says he is disobedient in the best sense, for being his own man when it comes to writing.

I love to watch a storm approaching across the fields and over Burgate Wood, with the dark backdrop of sky rolling up, and the willows and ash trees still lit up by the sun close by, so they glow and radiate the brightness of their winter architecture. Here I am in my study at half past nine in the morning with the electric light on, and two pullovers.

The Whole Earth Catalogue, our bible as self-builders of our residences in the hippie-ish days of the 1970s, was subtitled 'access to tools'. 'With tools,' ran the editorial preface, 'you can do more or less anything.'

Buckminster Fuller weighed in at the front with an encouraging piece about geodesic domes, and a movement was launched all over the world. They showed the earth as a tiny planet on the front cover, as photographed from space.

Tools were what we needed, and tools were what we went out and sought. I went to farm auctions and bought impossibly long wooden stack ladders nobody needed or wanted any more for a few pounds. I bought a giant 1948 Fordson Major tractor with a six-cylinder Perkins diesel engine in perfect working order, and a full armoury of ploughs, harrows, cultivators and hay-cutters to go with it, for well under £600.

Something is eating a leaf. Everything is so still I can hear it – like my rabbits in their cage in the morning before school, chewing on the hogweed I collected along the lane. The moat is frozen. Leaves are frozen in it like ash in amber. There's a slight smokiness under the ice where water flows in through a dyke. Chirruping of magpies, scolding, tut-tutting of blackbirds.

Very bright blue frosty day. Moat and ponds properly frozen for the first time this year.

In Burgate Wood. Dozens of squirrels scamper off across the ride. Clattering of dry brown oak leaves falling like snow.

Huge old cratered coppice stools of hazel, hornbeam and maple. A hornbeam stool has collapsed, spreadeagled on the wood floor like a starfish.

Pulmonaria patch. Hornbeam with thirteen stems. Moat is dry round the banked manor site. Dead hornbeam leaves. Hazels on the site, dead nettle stems, coppiced ash and hazel and oak, remains of an old causeway. Walking along the bottom of the moat. Shrivelled dog's mercury. Stumps, like rocks, mossed, lichens.

Sudden 'sinking' into moat. Huge coppice ash, cratered coppice maple, ten feet across the wandering stool. Snail shells amongst dead leaves. Rabbits bolting through wood. Sudden shocking pink of spindle-tree fruit.

What kind of freedom is it to walk or to cycle on our roads if we are forced to wear luminous jackets like lifeboatmen in broad daylight?

Outside loo frozen up. Stopped down the mains tap and wedged up the cistern ballcock.

Christmas Eve. Rufus and I spend Friday in the snow and frost, wooding in the spinney beyond the round pond – old dead hawthorns that have crashed down in gales.

In the morning I walked out past the shepherd's hut in the snow and up flew two cock pheasants (arguing), a magpie and a wood pigeon.

Walnuts. Open a walnut and something very like a brain drops out.

A walnut boat in the bath with a sail.

It's funny, you read someone like T. H. White for an hour in the early morning and your mind grooves on to him and you find yourself writing away downhill as if guided and balanced by his invisible hand at your elbow. You don't have to even think about a thing. Just push off and freewheel.

'Then, when I am dead, they must bury me in a bend of the river, like Colonel Leslie.' What does it mean, the bend in the river? Why might a place at the bend of a river, in the crook of its twisting, be regarded as sacred? Is it that the river contains it somehow? Why would the river choose to kink itself at such a place? Perhaps because of some special power in it. Some force field.

27th December

Snow, early morning, settled on everything. Trees sugared and frosted. Tracks (a few morning pheasants and a feral cat) in the snow.

The hedge in the long meadow casts shadows of shelter: marginally warmer spots, protected from the chill of the wind, where the snow doesn't settle so much and where the grass remains green and the molehills brown. I looked for blewits but found none.

This is the one moment when you can be in a wood alone, and know for certain you are alone, because there are no other tracks but yours.

30th December

The very act of writing at this time of year is a ritual re-affirmation of life to come in the longer, lighter days, like the lighting of a Yule log. The phoenix – flame of the imagination.

The very presence of birds in the hazel tree by the moat presages spring, even though they're starving and in a state of deep dependence on the bird feeder I fill with peanuts every other day.

31st December

New Year's Eve walk.

Dad and I used to sing songs on our walks to keep the rhythm going. 'Ilkley Moor Baht' at'. 'John Brown's Body'.

At night you can see the parish boundary pear tree before you. It's not a real tree, just a shadow of another tree.

You look up at the stars and you're at sea, you're sailing. All round the common are the landlocked people, their lights winking from behind their curtains. They're stuck in front of their televisions, having their dinners, doing up their shoelaces, ironing, worrying about tomorrow, working on their computers, voyaging on the web. They're all far, far away from here, not navigating through the wind across the wide open sea of the common.

I watch the planes criss-crossing the night sky. Their lights are flashing; they're flying out of Mildenhall and Lakenheath. And a pond looms up like a mirage, just the dull reflection of the moon in it. The moon is also lying in a puddle, and the lit windows are reflected too.

'John Brown's body lies a-mouldering in the grave . . .'

Now, as I turn back along the common, the wind is at my back, and I am no longer battling it. All is suddenly quiet and peaceful, and the wind is no more than a gentle hand on my back. Clouds riding the wind under the stars and the orange glow of Diss beneath them as they cross the common. I hear a distant car approaching, make my way off the road on to the tussocky grass and move deeper into the darkness. As the head-lights swing round a bend behind me, I feel like a rabbit caught in the sudden sweep of light, and see my long straight extended shadow marching half a mile and more over the lit ground.

The car is slowing down. It's stopping. Why? Because it caught a glimpse of me as it rounded the corner and its head-light swept the common. Just a glimpsed figure far out in the open ground at dead of night. What is he thinking? I feel like a hunted animal. He just sits there, lights on, and keeps putting his foot down on the brake pedal – a nervous twitch? Now he moves off, slowly, as if undecided. I watch the lights recede.

I half trip in the softness of a molehill. A young owl twitters on a straggly hedgerow by a stream.

My overcoat is like a sail, with the wind driving me forward, the collar straight up like a ruff around my neck and the vulnerable back of the skull, a little button fastening it right up round my ears.

I'm following the dark brown line of a cow track. The sudden dazzle of headlights approaching me, radiating into a thousand icicles in the dark. A porcupine of light.

Puddles in the scuppers of the road. Pushed aside into the scuppers of the road. Drenched in the scuppers of the road as the car speeds by.

This wind is what an oak has to stand up to every night. A pair of big trees stand on the common outside Hall Farm. The poplar almost threadbare, the oak solid and substantial; the poplar trying to emulate the way the oak defies gravity with a long horizontal bough, but failing – the next really savage gale will probably tear it off. Now it stands like a matchstick, a scarecrow in torn rags.

A shooting star, and another shooting star.

Notes

Notes have been included only for those of Roger's friends who have work in the public domain which readers may wish to follow up.

JANUARY

p. 2 Ronald Blythe's books include *Akenfield: Portrait of an English Village* (1969), *Word from Wormingford* (1998) and *The Assassin* (2004).

p. 2 Dr 'Bird' Partridge, a psychiatrist who worked at the Maudsley Hospital in London, was a friend and neighbour of John Nash.

p. 3 John Nash (1893–1977), the English painter, illustrator and engraver, was an old friend of Ronald Blythe and, with his wife, was the previous owner of Bottengoms Farm.

p. 4 Jayne Ivimey is an artist who has specialized in capturing the East Anglian landscape and studying the issues affecting it.

p. 5 The work of artist Helen Napper, who lives in Suffolk, has been exhibited in London, New York and Santa Monica.

p. 9 A transmocho tree is one pollarded during its life to provide for the specific requirements of ship-building.

p. 14 Richard Jefferies, *At Home on the Earth*. Selected and introduced by Jeremy Hooker, Green Books (2001).

p. 15 Eddie Krutysza is the owner-manager of Hatton Farm Nurseries in Metfield, Suffolk.

p. 17 The writer and naturalist Richard Mabey's books include *Flora Britannica* (1996), *Nature Cure* (2005) and *Beechcombings: The Narrative of Trees* (2007).

p. 18 Colin Ward, *Cotters and Squatters: The Hidden History of Housing*, Five Leaves Publications (2002).

p. 19 The Robert Graves poem is 'Love without hope'.

p. 19 Tony Barrell is an award-winning documentary maker who lives in Australia. He is the author of *The Real Far East: Way Beyond Siberia* (2007) and, with Rick Tanaka, *Higher than Heaven: Japan, War and Everything* (1996) and *Okinawa Dreams OK* (1998).

p. 20 Geoffrey Household's classic thriller *Rogue Male* was one of Roger's favourite books. Published in 1939, it tells the story of an unnamed

Englishman who, having tried and failed to assassinate an unnamed German dictator, is tortured and then goes on the run from the dictator's henchmen in 'the green depths of Dorset'. Roger had heard that the exact location of the hollow-way where the hero of *Rogue Male* hid could be located in the Chideock Valley. He agreed with Rob Macfarlane (see note for page 41), who shared his enthusiasm's for Household's thriller, that they should go on a trip to test its description against the landscape. Macfarlane's account of the trip is included in his book *The Wild Places* (2007).

p. 21 The Canadian author Elizabeth Smart's affair with George Barker inspired her best-known work, *By Grand Central Station I Sat Down and Wept* (1945).

FEBRUARY

p. 23 John Middleton Murry (1889–1957) was a prominent literary critic and minor member of the Bloomsbury Group.

p. 26 Mike Dibb's documentaries include the influential BBC series *Ways of Seeing* (1972) and *The Miles Davis Story*, which was awarded an international Emmy in 2001 as arts documentary.

p. 26 David Nash, RA, is an internationally acclaimed sculptor who works mainly with wood. Roger's account of meeting him can be found in *Wildwood*.

p. 28 Terence Blacker's books include *Kill Your Darlings* (2000) and *You Cannot Live as I Have Lived and Not End Up Like This: The Disgraceful Life and Times of Willie Donaldson* (2006).

p. 37 Andrew Sanders is a film production designer whose credits include *The Witches* (1990), *The Golden Bowl* (2000), *Possession* (2002) and *The White Countess* (2005).

p. 38 Film director and writer Mike Hodges's work includes *Get Carter* (1971), *Croupier* (1998) and *I'll Sleep When I'm Dead* (2003).

p. 39 Ben Platts-Mills is a sculptor in wood who has public artworks sited in Suffok and Norfolk.

p. 41 Robert Macfarlane is the author of *Mountains of the Mind: A History of a Fascination* (2003) and *The Wild Places* (2007).

p. 41 For Roger's account of this trip, see pages 167–74.

p. 47 Kim Taplin, *Tongues in Trees: Studies in Literature and Ecology*, Green Books (1992).

p. 49 Eric Rolls, *Australia, A Biography: The Beginnings from the Cosmos to the Genesis of Gondwana, and its Rivers, Forests, Flora, Fauna and Fecundity*, University of Queensland Press (2000).

p. 49 Les Murray's collections of essays, which include *A Working Forest: Selected Prose* (1997) and *The Quality of Sprawl: Thoughts about Australia* (1999), are still not available from a British publisher.

MARCH

p. 57 An account of Roger's experience coppicing with his friend and neighbour Keith Dunthorne, a master thatcher, can be found in *Wildwood*.

p. 65 Alison Hastie, who was Roger's partner during the last years of his life, is the founder of the ethical footwear company Green Shoes.

APRIL

p. 68 Redgrave Fen, officially known as Redgrave and Lopham Fen, is a National Nature Reserve owned and run by the Suffolk Wildlife Trust.

p. 74 Derek Jarman (1942–94) was an eminent avant-garde film-maker and artist.

p. 80 *Microcosmos: Le Peuple de l'herbe* (1996), a documentary film directed by Claude Nuridsany and Marie Perénnou, revealed the lives of insects with startling and dramatic close-up photography.

p. 84 The artist Mary Newcomb (1922–2008) lived in Suffolk and Norfolk for over forty years. A chapter in *Wildwood* is devoted to her.

p. 91 W. G. Hoskins, *The Making of the English Landscape*, Hodder & Stoughton (1955). Oliver Rackham, *The History of the Countryside*, J. M. Dent (1986).

p. 97 E. F. Schumacher, *Small is Beautiful: A Study of Economics as if People Really Mattered*, Blond and Briggs (1973).

MAY

p. 102 The naturalist and explorer Charles Waterton (1782–1865) was author of *Wanderings in South America* (1825) and the three-volume *Essays on Natural History* (1838, 1844, 1857).

p. 105 Mike Westbrook, the jazz pianist and composer, was an old friend of Roger's.

p. 108 Gary Rowland is a designer and artist.

p. 110 The Australian broadcaster and author Ramona Koval, who presents *The Book Show* on ABC Radio National and whose books include *Tasting Life Twice – Conversations with Remarkable Writers* (2005), travelled through central Australia with Roger. His account of their journey can be found in *Wildwood*.

p. 120 Richard Flanagan's books include *Gould's Book of Fish* (2002) and *The Unknown Terrorist* (2007).

p. 122 The poet and translator Oliver Bernard's works include *Country Matters* (1961), *Rimbaud: Collected Poems* (1986) and his autobiography *Getting Over It* (1992).

p. 122 Tony Weston, one of Roger's oldest friends, is a potter and poet. His poetry collections include *Not for Cats* (1997) and *The Rainbow in the Bruise* (1998).

pp. 123–4 This poem was read by Roger at his uncle Frank Crook's birthday garden party in 2005.

p. 123 Wood was Roger's family name on his mother's side.

JUNE

p. 134 The twelfth-century church at Manaccan in Cornwall is renowned for the ancient fig tree which grows out of its walls.

p. 136 Henry David Thoreau, *A Week on the Concord and Merrimack Rivers* (1849).

p. 141 The folk singer-songwriter Steve Ashley has recorded nine solo albums, including the acclaimed *Stroll On* (1974). Roger was the subject of, and inspiration for, the song 'Friend of the Rivers' from his latest CD *Time and Tide* (2007).

p. 142 Iain Sinclair is the author of, among other books, *London Orbital* (2002) and *Dining on Stones* (2004) in which his journeys past Beckton Alp are discussed.

p. 147 Min Cooper is a cartoonist, illustrator and animator.

p. 149 Roger's great-uncle Joe Deakin, part of the group known as 'the Walsall anarchists', was arrested 6 January 1892 and charged with bomb-making. He stood trial with other alleged conspirators, was found guilty and jailed for five years. It was later discovered that the conspiracy had been instigated by a police *agent provocateur*.

p. 151 The line 'We were in love before we were introduced' comes from Patrick Kavanagh's poem 'On Reading a Book of Common Wild Flowers'.

JULY

p. 155 This reference is to Roger's days as an advertising copywriter. One of his lines, a famous slogan for the Coal Board, was 'Come home to a real fire.'

p. 160. The quotation is from the Russian writer Andrey Platonov (1899–1951).

pp. 162–3 The poet and gardener Alice Oswald's work includes her collections *The Thing in the Gap-Stone Stile* (1996), *Dart* (2002), which won the T. S. Eliot Prize, and *Woods etc* (2007).

p. 168 See note for page 20.

p. 168 Stephen Leather, *Tunnel Rats*, Hodder & Stoughton (1997).

p. 168 James Thurber, *The Thurber Carnival* (1945).

p. 174 The allusion to 'a ballista defensive front-line system' refers to the scene in *Rogue Male* (see note for page 20) in which the hero defends himself with a catapult, or ballista, constructed from cat-hide.

p. 174 W. H. Murray, *Mountaineering in Scotland* (1947).

p. 177 The novelist and screenplay writer Deborah Moggach's works include *Tulip Fever* (1999), *These Foolish Things* (2004) and *In the Dark* (2007).

p. 180 Tony Axon, a lifelong friend of Roger, is the founder and publisher of the World of Information reference series.

p. 180 Joe Deakin – see note for page 149.

p. 182 An account of Roger's meeting with the Australian artist and nomad John Wolseley is the subject of a chapter in *Wildwood* entitled 'At Leatherarse Gully'.

p. 183 The painter, illustrator and designer David Holmes worked with Roger during his advertising days and illustrated *Waterlog*, *Wildwood* and this book.

AUGUST

p. 187 The Great Ukulele Orchestra of Great Britain, an internationally known ukulele ensemble, was playing at the Snape Maltings.

p. 188 In August 2001, Mugabe's Zimbabwean army was reported to be ravaging the rainforest of the Congo with its logging operations.

p. 195 Barry Goater was Roger's biology teacher at Haberdashers' Aske's School and went on to write *The Butterflies and Moths of Hampshire and the Isle of Wight* (1974) and *British Pyralid Moths: A Guide to Their Identification* (1986). An account of Roger's reunion with him is to be found in *Wildwood*.

p. 198 *History of the Countryside*: see note for page 91.

p. 203 Francesca Greenoak and Clare Roberts, *Wildlife in the Churchyard: The Plants and Animals of God's Acre*, Little Brown (1993).

p. 206 In 1865, Thomas Hardy was given the job of overseeing the exhumation and relocation of gravestones to make way for the railway station. He arranged the tombstones around an ash tree in St Pancras churchyard. It is now known as 'the Hardy Tree'.

SEPTEMBER

pp. 218–19 *Dolomedes* is a species of spider which includes the rare Fen Raft Spider, *Dolomedes Plantarius*, to be found at Redgrave and Lopham Fen near Walnut Tree Farm.

p. 220 The writer W. G. Sebald (1944–2001) wrote *The Rings of Saturn* (1998), an evocative and discursive account of a walk across East Anglia. The translator was Michael Hulse.

p. 221 'Richard Deacon-like scrap metal' refers to the sculptor Richard Deacon who works in metal and wood.

p. 223 The 'pagodas' of Orford Ness are testing cells which were used for atomic bomb testing during the late 1950s and 1960s.

p. 235 Ivor Gurney (1890–1937), poet and composer.

OCTOBER

p. 237 'Barry Lopez-style' is a reference to the American nature writer Barry Lopez and his book *Of Wolves and Men* (1979).

p. 238 Wellington here is Wellington School, Hatch End.

p. 241 The writer and thinker Satish Kumar is the editor of the magazine *Resurgence*, for which Roger wrote regularly, and Director of Programmes of the Schumacher College at Dartington Hall. His books include *You Are, Therefore I Am: A Declaration of Dependence (2002)* and *Spiritual Compass: The Three Qualities of Life* (2007).

p. 243 'Swinger of birches': this phrase is from Robert Frost's poem 'Birches'.

p. 246 W. G. Sebald: see note for page 220.

p. 247 Puzzle Wood is a 14-acre ancient woodland in the Forest of Dean.

p. 252 Barry Goater: see note for page 195.

p. 262 The zoologist Desmond Morris's work includes *The Naked Ape* (1967) and *Watching: Encounters with Humans and Other Animals* (2006).

NOVEMBER

p. 269 *Touching Wood* was the working title for the project that became *Wildwood*.

p. 272 The author Adam Nicholson's books include *Sea Room: An Island Life in the Hebrides* (2001) and *Earls of Paradise* (2008).

p. 281 Peter Randall-Page is a sculptor whose large-scale commissions have been exhibited internationally.

p. 282 The composer and musician Harvey Brough's work includes *Requiem in Blue* (1999) and *Valete in Pace* (2004). With Clara Sanabras, he formed the band *Clara and the Real Lowdown*, whose first CD was released in 2008.

p. 284 Roger's account of his experience at Hell Gill can be read in *Waterlog*.

DECEMBER
p. 296 *The Whole Earth Catalogue* was the ultimate reference work for the counter-culture and has been described as an early forerunner of internet search engines. It was published twice a year between 1968 and 1972 and occasionally thereafter. The last edition was in 1998.

Acknowledgements

The editors would like to thank Rufus Deakin for giving them access to his father's papers, and to express their gratitude to Roger's literary executor Robert Macfarlane and his agent Georgina Capel for their support and encouragement throughout this project. Roger's friends Tony Axon, Jules Cashford, Vicky Minet and Tony and Bundle Weston have provided invaluable advice and insights. Thanks are also due to Jack Sturgess for his reading of the final manuscript. The heroic task of typing up handwritten entries from the notebooks was achieved by Dianne Hood.

Once again David Holmes's superb illustrations have been a perfect compliment to Roger's writing.

The efficiency and enthusiasm of those working on the book at Hamish Hamilton has been exemplary. Special thanks go to Simon Prosser who commissioned and championed it, to Debbie Hatfield who oversaw its progress, and to Donna Poppy for her sympathetic and scrupulous line-editing.